Stony Ridge School, 1939.

Spatzies and Brass BBs

Life in a One-Room Country School

DR. KEN OHM

LEATHERS
PUBLISHING

Photos on pages i, 16 and 214 are from the Walter M. Andersen Collection, Emporia State University Libraries and Archives, Emporia, Kansas. Photos on pages 5, 9, 24, 33, 42, 46, 64, 73, 79, 85, 88, 94, 139, 148, 166 and 181 are by Brenda Culbertson. The front and back cover photos are by Brenda Culbertson and feature Stach School on the grounds of the Kansas Museum of History. Further Stach School photos are on pages 5, 24, 64 and 88. All other photos are provided by the author.

Sketches on pages 12, 27, 36, 53, 56, 59, 62, 68, 76, 91, 98, 110, 111, 127, 156, 160, 163 and 206 are by Rachel Sager/Pink Dress Productions.

Second printing December 2004.

ISBN 1-58597-278-9 (soft cover edition)
ISBN 1-58597-289-4 (hard cover edition)

Library of Congress Control Number: 2004094274

A division of Squire Publishers, Inc.
4500 College Blvd.
Leawood, KS 66211
1/888/888/7696
www.leatherspublishing.com

ACKNOWLEDGMENTS

To Mom and Dad, the two heroes in my life. Their tireless effort to provide for their family is a daily memory.

My special thanks and admiration goes to Mr. Don Pady. Apart from his generous contribution of time and energy in guiding me through this project, he has become a valued friend.

My wife, Ruth, has been a patient ally and an inspiration to me to complete this book. I have been motivated by my children, Jeni, Gary, Kelly and Robert, to provide a lasting glimpse into their father's early life which will hopefully be shared with grandchildren, Julie, Ryan, Sean, Kevin, Dallas, Ariel, Lacey and Garrett.

My sister, Bonnie, and my friend, Adrienne Halpin, read and generously commented on the complete manuscript. They helped shape and focus the writing, offered fresh ideas and pointed out where the narrative could be improved. Further, their encouragement was invaluable.

The staff at the Kansas Museum of History and Max Krause at the Anderson Museum in Emporia, Kansas provided valuable and enthusiastic assistance.

Also, for their professionalism, constructive comments and support, special credit goes to my publisher, Tom Leathers, and book manager, Mollie Eulitt.

TABLE OF CONTENTS

PREFACE

All that remains on the two sites of my former one-room, rural schools is a scattering of small concrete fragments from their foundations. During the last 60 years, the areas have been beaten down to ground level by grazing cattle and by wind, rain and snow. Sunnyside School was located in southern Kansas near the Oklahoma border, and provided an average facility and a basic education to its seven or eight students. Stony Ridge School, a hundred miles to the north, had barely the resources to keep the doors open for only three or four students. In both cases, a single classroom composed the entire school with outdoor toilets and no running water or electricity.

Despite these difficulties, the school boards of each school still managed to find a dedicated, sympathetic and caring teacher. The classrooms were safe and friendly, but the educational process required discipline and rigor. We had a great opportunity to develop an imagination, to daydream and to think. Our days and nights were not filled with media noise — only wind, rain, birds, coyotes and our own thoughts.

My earlier childhood memories are sketchy, but with the first day of my first grade, I began a three-year period with as vivid a recollection as in any similar period in my life. With school in session for only seven or eight months a year, and with illnesses and bad weather further limiting attendance, real life outside the school occupied much of the students' attention and time. With life at Sunnyside centered on my father — who worked long hours in the oil fields — our home was peaceful and content. We had modern plumbing and electricity and a gas furnace. Always at home, Mom gave my sister and me her undivided attention. But after one year at Sunnyside, our lives dramatically changed when we moved north to Mom's childhood farm and added my grandfather as a member of our immediate family.

My new school, Stony Ridge, bore close likeness to Sunnyside, but living conditions at our new home provided a sharp contrast to life on the oil-lease. We had no running water, no indoor bathroom, and no electricity. To make a living on only 160 acres of land required a team effort. My sister and I soon took on chores every morning and evening, and we helped in any way we could to provide the family's basic needs. The combined stresses on my parents and grandfather must have been enormous, but their steady work and devotion never wavered. We quickly learned the reality of slaughtering animals for food and market, tending sick and aging animals, and killing other animals to protect our own or to make money. Although this quickly became routine, perhaps my life-long love for the peacefulness of schools was heightened by the alternative of hard physical labor and harsh reality.

Doing chores every day of the week, helping out with farm work and going to school occupied most of our time. On Sundays and holidays, however, most of our relatives visited us on the farm. We had 18 uncles and aunts and 29 cousins on Mom's side of the family. Playtime was an adventure and provided memories that have lasted a lifetime. These educational and life experiences provided me with an unshakable basis for my academic life as a student, professor and college dean.

The accounts that follow are prominent in my memory. Even after 60 or more years, they are, to me, as real and factual as if they occurred yesterday. I hope this story will provide a glimpse into wartime lives in tiny one-room schools across the country. The years described here are just the beginning of my life story, but they still reflect an almost daily recall of one event or another from those impressionable times.

Dr. Ken Ohm
Fall, 2004
Ken.Ohm@Washburn.edu
Topeka, Kansas

❧ 1 ❧

The First Day of School

I pull the bed sheets over my head as the sun comes through the bedroom window. "Kenny, it's time to get up for school," Mom shouts. I jump out of bed and notice Dad leaning against the doorway, grinning broadly. He normally works at this time of the morning, so this must be a very special day! Mom helps me put on my shirt, socks and pants. I next put on my shoes, and down my Malt-O-Meal with cream and sugar. Mom combs my hair and hands me my lunch bucket. Dad is waving goodbye as we step out the door and into the car.

After more than 60 years, my memory is like brilliant sunlight. Mom had just dropped me off at the tiny one-room country school about a mile from our house. It was supposed to be a matter-of-fact experience as I walked alone up to the front door clutching my Karo Syrup lunch bucket. Several kids ran around in the field to the west. As I hesitantly approached the open door, the teacher met me and greeted me so warmly I almost forgot that Mom had just left. She took my bucket and placed it on a shelf in the tiny cloakroom and introduced herself as Miss Dalton. I found out later that she was just 19 years old, but she certainly appeared to have things under control. After she showed me my desk at the front of the room, she suggested that I go out and join the other

1

kids. I barely got to the playground when her hand bell sounded and I followed the kids back inside.

It was nice to know exactly where I was going as I made my way to the front row. All the desks were designed for just one student and had seats attached at the front for students in the next row ahead. As the youngest student, I was seated in front of the room. The seat on the front of my desktop gave the teacher numerous opportunities to sit sideways and help me with my work. This was a delightful time for me, and Miss Dalton always greeted me with a sincere and happy smile. Trying to adjust my freestanding desk was not difficult with no one in front of me. I had to be careful, however, not to move my seat too much, as it would bother the student behind me. Since we only had a few students in the school, each was assigned an alternate desk, side by side. It made visiting between students a bit more difficult, but apparently one student behind the other was not much of a problem.

Once seated, Miss Dalton asked us all to stand and recite the Pledge of Allegiance. I did not know the words, so I had to just stand there while the rest of the students recited loudly. Later in the day, I was instructed by some of the older students on placing the hand over the heart and reciting the words of the pledge. After the pledge, Miss Dalton introduced me to the students and they were introduced to me.

We had a total of seven students on that first day — I was the only new one, and represented the entire first and second grade. Roger was a third grader and became as close to a real friend as I had in the school. Two fourth-grade girls were best friends, and I never got to know them very well. The fifth-grader was a boy and a loner and had attendance problems throughout the school year.

The other two students were Norman and Mary. Both in the eighth grade, they seemed as old as the teacher. While pleasant and conversant with me, they offered no real friendship. They seemed to be ready to move on impatiently with their last year and head out into the real world.

The older kids knew from the first day what to do with their schoolwork, and this routine would soon become familiar to me, also. Each day's instruction began when the teacher said a few words to them before they immediately began to read and write. I was handed a first grade reader shortly after the introductions, and Miss Dalton stood over my left shoulder pointing to the first word on the first page, "Wee." This story about a little mouse was to be my entry into the world of reading and academics. We had never read at home before my school days, so this was an entirely new experience. She described the meaning of that first word, and I have often thought how infrequently I have encountered it during my lifetime. But what an incredible experience it was to actually see a printed word and understand its related meaning! With the teacher helping me for several minutes that day — and during the next two or three days — I soon recognized and read all of the words of that story.

The first day's morning just flew by! Lunchtime was delightful, and I eagerly ate from my lunch pail for the first time. It was an incredibly new experience to be away from home or from a parent for more than an hour or two. I could just feel the freedom of body and spirit. After we finished lunch, we could go outside to play. Three or four kids greeted me on an improvised baseball field. A large flat rock served as home plate, and a rusty disk from a farm implement simulated a single base. With only a few kids playing, the goal was to hit the pitched ball and run to the base and back to home before a fielder could either throw in front of the runner or hit the runner to put him out. If you outran the ball in either case, you could continue to bat. The rules for this game of "work-up" were very consistent, and the older kids enforced them. Fly balls caught in the air were outs, as were three strikes. All foul balls were counted as strikes.

I started the game in the outfield as the youngest player, although I didn't get a chance to field the ball. I did get to toss a few pitches underhand, and the batter was put out. I soon worked my way up to bat and learned how to hold and swing it. One of the kids emphatically showed me how it should be done, and I managed to hit the first pitch — but was thrown out. The "kitten-ball" we used was much larger than a typical softball of today. When hit, the impact of bat against ball created a considerable vibration in the hands and arms. It took strength and accuracy to throw it across the field, but it was quite soft and not dangerous if it hit someone.

About then, my mom drove up in the old '32 Chevy. She smiled broadly as she stopped nearby and asked how I liked school. My reply has been relayed back to me during my entire life — from Mom, Dad and sister Bonnie. I said, "I like it so well, I don't know what to do." This must have been a foretelling of my lifetime ahead with school and teaching occupying my 46-year professional life. I told Mom that I had to go and quickly ran back to the "diamond." She saw that things were going well and drove off for home.

The afternoon went by quickly and, after the most exciting day in my young life, Mom picked me up at school and drove me home. This was probably the last time I had a ride to or from school. From that time on, I would always walk, both ways.

A seat for Miss Dalton.

The old school bell.

2

The Walks to School

I have already been up for almost two hours doing chores, eating breakfast and getting dressed. When the clock reads eight, I grab my lunch pail and walk out the door. My thoughts are mostly on getting to school on time, and I try not to delay myself by the sights and sounds along the way.

There were no buses for country students. Schools had to be built close enough to allow for a reasonable walking distance. My home was over a mile away, so these walks were an adventure. The trek from home to school was rich in all kinds of attractions. We loved the colors of autumn, the changing sights and sounds of birds and other game animals throughout the winter months and — the most delightful time of all — spring. To walk out into the bright, fresh, green countryside and hear the song of the meadowlark provided a feeling of new life.

We usually took the gravel road around a section of land; some days we headed directly across the fields. Before school started in the early fall, Dad attached a large, very heavy log to a team of horses to drag through the fields on the way to school. This technique gouged a shallow pathway through the high weeds and provided a shorter walk during good weather. Our walks to and from school were, for the most part, deliberate. Since we had chores to do, and since school started precisely at 9 a.m., being late at either end of the walk was not tolerated by the teacher or by the parents. We were not allowed on the school grounds until 8:45 a.m. If we arrived early, we had to stand on the side of the main road in front of the school. If we arrived late, we were not allowed into the school until after the first recess. We could not play on the school grounds after school. But, if we had to stay after school to consult with the teacher, it would seldom take longer than one-half hour. This was in respect for the student's responsibilities at home. Any disruption in this routine would startle our parents at home — by whom some kind of discipline was enforced. Sometimes fellow students would wait down the road for the detained student to catch up with them.

The next school day would undoubtedly bring another walk regardless of the weather conditions. When the mud on the roads or in the fields was too heavy, our feet occasionally pulled out of one or both of our four-buckle overshoes. We also lost our balance a number of times and stepped into the mud with our regular shoes, or in some cases, our socks. After a step or two to retrieve the overshoes, we had quite a mess that required lots of cleaning. We were expected to help with that job, but Mom or the teacher did most of it. The final stage of cleanup was placing both socks and shoes near the kitchen stove, or the school stove, to dry out.

As we walked through the cornfields in the late fall, we would stop and pull aside one of the vertical corn shocks which had been stacked together. This left an opening inside — similar to, we guessed, an Indian tee-pee — and gave us a little place to "hide and pretend."

Walking to school on the gravel roads also provided an introduction to my lifelong passion for throwing things. I would throw rocks each day at my targets of telephone poles standing at regular intervals on one side of the road. Although tempted, I never threw at the glass insulators on the cross bars at the top of the poles. My dad made it very clear that if I broke one it would interfere with our haphazard telephone system and I would really "catch it" at home. I never doubted this for a moment. I did, however, aim at numerous birds on the wires between the poles, and over the period of nearly three years of daily walking, managed to hit a few of them. Those events were not very happy ones and later, when my younger sister was walking with me, she would reprimand me for it. For some reason, she never reported this behavior to our parents. She probably realized that these direct hits were so few and far between that the chance of another hit was very low.

With a developing arm, my early rock throwing provided me the strength to become a baseball pitcher some years later when we moved to town. I continued pitching throughout high school and college. Although I had every intention of playing big-league baseball, I injured my arm during my junior year in college — and so I concentrated on other sports such as tennis and skiing until I reached age 55. I then qualified to participate in senior track meets. Having thrown the javelin successfully in high school, I chose to give it another try. I eventually reached All-American status in my 66th year, while participating in meets all over the country and ranked in the top four in the United States and top 20 in the world. This achievement, according to some experts, could be attributed to those happy days when I threw rocks as I walked to and from school.

A tempting target.

3

Clodhoppers and Overalls

It is Monday morning and I crawl out of bed reaching for my overalls. Since they came off the clothesline just last night, they are not only cold, but really stiff. I finally get my legs into them, but it is going to take some time to get them loosened up. Mom said I could wear my flannel shirt for another week since it wasn't very dirty. As I put it on, it really feels good on my skin and I warm up quickly.

The preparations for each school day started the previous evening with Mom's attempt to get the proper clothes together. The actual appearance of the clothes was quite unimportant as they were chosen to provide warmth and comfort, not style or fashion. With families having little differences in resources, most students wore hand-me-downs. Many families had more than one student in the school at the same time, and although their clothes may have been recognized, they were never mentioned as being worn by someone else. Since I wore pretty much the same clothes day after day, the primary difference was with layering. In the early winter's first cold spell, itchy woolen underwear was un-packed from the dresser drawer. They often smelled of mothballs after being stored for several months. Both boys and girls wore these red or white "longies" even though they were very uncomfortable. The "trap door" in the lower back made it possible to carry on daily requirements without taking them off. Many kids wore the same "long-johns" night and day for a full week or more. Both body and clothes washing took place on weekends, and, for most of the kids, the same clothes would show up again and again, week after week.

The girls wore gingham dresses most of the time with under-garments determined by the weather. They often wore long stockings over their underwear in the winter. The boys, without exception, wore blue bib-overalls. They provided front-and back-pockets for knives and handkerchiefs and a full-front breast pocket for pencils and a number of other items. These items included marbles, willow whistles, toads and small snakes. Our shoes were called "clodhoppers" and were worn on cold days, and occasionally, in the fields in summer. They were high-topped leather and laced with leather shoestrings. For the most part, kids went barefooted for eight or nine months each year. It would take the first frost to get shoes on some of the kids as they walked to and from school.

Mittens, with a thumb only, were worn during very cold weather. Just as today, we had a hard time keeping track of them at home and at school. Much later in my childhood — when I got my first pair of five-finger gloves — I remember how much colder my hands were, when wearing them. What was gained in dexterity was lost in warmth when the fingers were not in direct contact with each other. Stocking caps were worn all during the cold winter season. We wore no hats in summer unless we spent a full day in the cornfield. Then, we needed a straw hat — along with a red bandana or kerchief around the neck.

Year-around wear.

❧ 4 ❧

The Oil Lease

If I lie perfectly still in my bed, I can hear my parents talking in the kitchen. Even though they are talking in German, I just love to hear their voices. I can tell that Dad is talking very seriously, in his low voice, probably about the war and the chances that he will be leaving us soon to go to war. Mom listens and responds quietly, likely assuring Dad that we will get along just fine and he need not worry. Thank goodness Mom will always be with us!

I turned seven years old in December of 1943. World War II was in full force and we lived in fear that Dad would soon be called to serve in the army. He had been deferred as a vital member in the oil supply business as it was one of the few occupations that allowed deferment during this time of extreme national crisis. Whether aware of his status or whether he felt guilty for not serving in the armed forces, he was determined to do his job to help his country. No man ever worked harder and had longer hours. He began work before I awakened in the morning, about five or five-thirty, and usually came home after dark as my sister and I were getting ready for bed. We only had time for a few words with him, but we always looked forward to it. He said that he was born old and I really can't remember seeing him look young

— even though he was only about 36 years old at this time.

We had a house on an oil lease near Winfield, Kansas — just a few miles from the Oklahoma border. It was a fairly modern home with indoor plumbing, a bathroom and a gas-cooking stove. With the constant fear of storms, we hand-dug a cellar several yards to the east of the house. It was supplied with a small bed and a kerosene lamp. My sister and I were carried out many nights when the wind would rise with approaching thunder, lightning and dark clouds.

The oil-field workers made rounds by foot, from one oilrig to another, both day and night, checking for equipment problems and hand-cranking the large engines to restart them. I walked with Dad several times to some of the rigs and marveled at how complicated these large structures were and the incredible amount of physical labor required of the oil field workers.

Most of the kids at Sunnyside School had fathers or other relatives working for the oil company. On occasion, we all had the opportunity to see an oil well "come in." This was anticipated for weeks after the geologists confirmed that they had found oil on the site. When the gusher would be near, the wait would start and families of the oil workers would gather at the site in their cars. We might never see our fathers for several days as it was generally a 24-hour-a-day process to drill the final few feet down to the treasure. It was a party-time atmosphere with family automobiles circling the oilrig and picnic lunches spread out on blankets on the nearby ground. The smell of deviled eggs and fried chicken drifted over the whole scene.

On one particular evening, at sunset, the workers excitedly yelled that the oil was on its way to the top of the ground. Everyone scrambled to quickly wrap the food and dishes in their blan-

14

kets and carry them to their car. With a great explosion of sound, the oil burst from the ground to heights greater than the seventy-foot oilrig. The workers were clear of the actual hole, but close enough so that when the oil came back down it drenched them. Depending on a car's location, it might be covered with oil as well. A light mist of oil landed on our car, and we cleaned our windshields with great difficulty before our trip home.

After the gusher, the workers rushed in and, within a short time, were able to contain the surging oil and normalize the operation. During the next several days, the site was cleaned up and fresh dirt was brought in to cover the heaviest areas of residual oil. The new well would eventually come "on-line," and the mood of everyone involved was elevated when their incredible efforts were finally rewarded. I had never known Dad happier and more self-confident than during these times.

Expecting a gusher!

🌿 5 🌿

The School House

As I crest the final hill on my daily walk, the school sits high against a cold, gray sky. I turn left off the gravel road and pass the opening in the fence and onto the school grounds. The timing of my arrival to the school grounds is good today, so I don't have to wait outside. I walk directly into the school. It probably isn't dark enough to have the lamps lit, but I can sure smell the kerosene. It would be so nice to lighten the day.

Both country schools I attended during my first three years of public education showed many similarities. Located some one hundred miles apart, the oil-lease school named Sunnyside was a few miles north of Winfield, Kansas, and Stony Ridge school was a few miles southwest of Olpe, Kansas. Both were wood frame buildings built in the 1870s. The inside walls and ceiling had plaster coatings and the roof had wood shingles. Mortar for the foundation held a mixture of sand and lime with horsehair used to bind it all together. The dimensions of both schools measured about 18'x25'; but the Sunnyside school, with a small entryway or cloakroom, had a smaller classroom area. The entry to the Stony Ridge School was directly from the outside where a few benches were placed inside the door for lunch boxes and overshoes. Hooks were provided on the walls above the benches for coats and hats. Neither school had electricity, telephones, running water, plumbing nor indoor bathroom facilities. Both had three kerosene lamps about six feet above the floor along each of the long walls. These lamps lighted the room for evening gatherings and illuminated especially dark rooms on rare cloudy days. We could always smell kerosene as it evaporated from the lamps into the room.

Both schools stood on non-arable land — close to situated roads. The Sunnyside School lay on flat, treeless land, surrounded on three sides by pastureland with a gravel road in front. The hand-dug well for drinking water had an iron hand pump. The Stony Ridge School stood on a high point of a gently-sloped hill with rock protruding from all three sides of cattle pasture. It also had a gravel road in front. Run-off rainwater provided its water supply and was collected into a cistern — cranked up with a handle attached to a series of metal cups. Either the teacher or one of the kids would carry in a bucket of water at the beginning of each school day for drinking and hand-washing. The metal water bucket stood on a table near the door, and the warm water always had a murky smell and taste. We had only one dipper for all the kids, each taking no more than we could drink. Unused water was never put back into the bucket. A washbasin of water warmed on or near the stove each day alongside a bar of homemade lye soap and a single, cotton towel used by all. The last in line to wash one's hands was almost a lost cause since the dirty water would be very dark by that time.

The six-foot diameter round cistern had a cover which was opened only a few times during the year. This cover kept out varmints of all kinds, including mice and snakes. When opened, one could usually see a layer of very fine dust or silt trapped on

18

the bottom from when water had run off a dusty roof. This was never any real concern since the cups only dipped into the upper level of the water pool. On rare occasions, especially in the early fall, run-off water was not sufficient. When this happened, one of the parents would have to make the trip into Olpe, some ten miles away, to haul water back to fill the cistern. The containers for these few hundred gallons were supplied by one of the neighbors — as, on occasion, they had to carry water to supply cattle during times of drought.

In the late summer, before the beginning of the school term, the school board would offer a $10 salary to anyone who would clean the schoolhouse. This included a full floor to ceiling scrubbing, window washing, and — perhaps the greatest challenge of all — draining and cleaning the cistern. Since it was difficult for most adults to get down to the floor of the cistern, children would frequently take the job. A chlorine and water mix was used to scrub down the inside and floor, using brooms and rags. Rarely did the same people accept the cleaning job from one year to the next.

When entering either school, the first thing noticed at the front was a large picture of George Washington and one of Abraham Lincoln. These classic prints were found in most one-room rural schools of the time. Both schools had a single slate blackboard that reached across the wall behind the teacher's desk. We had an eraser or two, but we usually erased the boards with cotton rags.

The desks measured the same size with simple style and with no drawers or storage space. The younger students had more difficulty sitting at the correct height, and some boosted their height by sitting on textbooks. Although the teacher had a chair behind her desk, I recall few times, in either classroom, when the chair was used during class time. Before and after school hours, and sometimes during recess or noon-hour, she would sit and look over papers and plan lessons. Often, she would walk among the students checking and correcting their work and, while standing, listen to recitations. With older kids reciting lessons within earshot of the younger ones, various topics were covered several times for each student over a period of years. This provided a real advantage for the learning process in a tiny one-room school.

The Sunnyside School had single desks while the Stony Ridge School had doubles. In both cases, there were several more desks than were needed because enrollment in the early '40s was down considerably from the previous decade. It proved impossible to earn a living on many of the smaller farms, and the schools had to consolidate into larger ones. The desks had pencil grooves near the top of the writing surface and a hole to the right for an inkwell. Some of the desks had a brass insert, with a flip lid to cover the inkwell, while others still had the beautiful purple glass ink jar sitting in the hole. Only a few of these were used in my time, when special occasions required ink lettering and were completed by the teacher. The Stony Ridge teacher, Miss Bechtel, would then use one of the old pens to provide a stylized exhibition of a special penmanship and lettering. This special form of writing style, or writing hand, had pretty much disappeared by the time I started school. But my father also had it — and what a pleasure it was to read his letters over the years! He was very fond of handwriting, and he practiced his penmanship during free moments throughout his lifetime.

Stony Ridge as it is now. Located on a farm about 15 miles to the east of its former location, it is now a grain bin, half-full of corn with boarded windows. Its drooping roof and peeling paint hide the echoes of its hundreds of former students.

⚜ 6 ⚜

The Pot-Bellied Stove

I sure hope Miss Dalton has the stove started today. As I enter the school building, after my long walk, I smell fresh smoke and see the teacher at her desk. What a relief! Norman got here first and helped get the fire started, so I take off my coat and walk to my desk at the front of the room.

The stove was the focal point in both schools. It warmed the school, dried wet clothes and heated water. It was wood or coal-burning, about four feet high and accurately described as "pot-bellied." For students close to the stove, the heat could rise to become nearly unbearable, while at the far corners of the room the temperature could fall to almost freezing.

The Sunnyside School had its stove near the front of the room and to the teacher's right, while the Stony Ridge stove was at the back of the room near the entry door. With the Sunnyside stove near the front and the chimney in the back, a long stove pipe extended all the way across the ceiling, allowing more heat to escape into the classroom. The Stony Ridge chimney, on the other hand, was directly over the stove with less efficiency, but perhaps it provided a little more safety.

With the teacher also serving as janitor, the bigger boys assisted by carrying in the coal and kindling or corncobs for the fire. If the kindling were damp, they brought it inside the school building the previous day — or else a little of the lamp kerosene might be needed to help start the fire. Controlling heat was achieved by regulating the airflow with a damper in the blackened tin stovepipe leading to the chimney. If the teacher or an older boy were skilled enough, it was sometimes possible to have yesterday's glowing coals left over to start the new day's fire. With skill and luck, the fire might even be "banked" to last over the weekend.

Today, with so much concern over fire safety, we might remember those old stoves as a serious hazard. Even though several country schools in Kansas had burned down and some kids killed, the over-all fire safety improved when the teacher explained what to do in an emergency. We had some drill instruction on how to escape through windows and assist the little kids in the process. The windows conveniently had no screens and were easily opened to the outside. In early spring, when the windows were first opened, the smells and sounds from outside filled the room and previewed that wonderful summer coming upon us.

The lower windows provided some needed heat relief during most of the school year. With warm weather in early fall or late spring, however, we tried to lower the top sash, as well. Since the windows generally were set quite high, to lessen distractions to the students, we needed to have a pole with a metal hook to slip into the top of the upper window. Pulling down on the pole would lower the upper window and give much needed relief from the stored heat near the ceiling.

The center of our room.

7

The Outhouse, the Horse Stall and the Coal Shed

I should not have drunk that extra cup of hot chocolate before I left for school this morning. Class has just started and already I need to go to the toilet. If I raise my arm and show one finger, the other kids will know what I want to do — and Miss Dalton will have to decide if I really need to go or not. My gosh, look outside. It's snowing. I would not be making this up!

On the outside of these one-acre rural school grounds stood two outhouses and one small combination coal shed and horse stall. In both schools, we had one or two students who rode horses every day and tied them up in the stall. Norman, the eighth grader at Sunnyside, rode several different horses during the year and prided himself with his horsemanship. When he would arrive at school, he would tie the reins to the hitching rack with a flair that filled the other kids with envy.

Farmers occasionally supplied hay or straw for the horses, but their feeding and watering at the school was not a priority and was provided exclusively by the children. Both stalls provided some protection from the north wind and from the sun, but the sides and entrance were open. The coal shed was built on the north side of the stall, and besides storing coal, it also held kindling wood and corncobs to help start the morning fire. Sometimes when the coal was a little wet and difficult to light, cobs were soaked with kerosene and added to the mix to get the fire started.

Kids often found the coal shed a good place to hide during games at recess. Occasionally, a brave boy would steal a kiss or put his arm around a girl in the dark quiet of the coal shed. On the other hand, one could expect lots of mice, skunks, gophers and a few snakes in the shed.

The outhouses on the Sunnyside grounds were right next to each other with a common path to them. The Stony Ridge out-houses were well apart with the girls on the northeast of the prop-erty and the boys on the northwest. Only one stall was included in each outhouse and had catalogs and newspapers to use instead of roll paper. It was not unusual for the kids to raise either one or two fingers to convince the teacher of the need to go to the out-side toilet, especially in the early warm days of spring. Since there was no heat whatsoever in the outhouses, I have never been colder as I visited them on zero-degree mornings.

Some of the neighbors eventually installed inside plumbing; but it was interesting to observe that when the weather was warm or the grounds muddy, most outdoor toilets continued to be used. It had become a regular habit to use the outdoor facilities, and kids, especially, found them much more convenient than going inside.

The outhouse.

8

Books, Etc.

Class has just begun and I notice that Mary has a new pencil box on her desk. When recess comes, I am going to ask her about it. Maybe she will talk to me. All I have are two pencils, which are already pretty short, and a thin Big Chief tablet. Boy, is she pretty!

The Register of Deeds in the two counties of my one-room schools provided a fascinating glimpse of how things were administered during those war years. As an example, one of the yearly reports shows total money expended for supplies was exactly $9.19. In another annual report, the "cost of books purchased during the year ending June 20, 1945" was $7.08. This same yearly report showed a total of $31.19 for "Light, power, fuel and water." And it revealed zero dollars for "Janitor's salary and supplies" and only $6.20 for "Maintenance on grounds, building, furniture, etc."

Although the 1945 report did not show the teacher's salary, the previous year's reported salary was $706.13 and included a "retirement deduction." Two years later, in 1947, the reported teacher salary and retirement deduction showed an increase to $1206.10. The "Length of term in days actually taught" varied between 150 and 160 days or seven and a half months to eight months.

One of the reports reflected the assessed valuation of the district as $310,626 and, by paying an annual premium of $32.32, insured the school building for $800.00. To establish the school census, persons over the age of five and under the age of twenty-one were counted and verified by a parent or guardian. The number in each grade — categorized by "Males or Females" and "White or Colored" — was totaled; yet the reports showed only about 30% of the school census actually enrolled in the school. The rest of the students were over 14 years old and attended high school or did not attend any school. Although not as prevalent as in my parents' time, one or two of the older kids did not show up for school before October and would be gone again by early April. They were either needed on the farm by their parents, or perhaps convinced them that they were needed. Some of the older kids at sixteen or so would struggle with fifth-grade work because of their absences during the previous years.

For the most part, the only new supplies we used during the school year were writing tablets and pencils that each student purchased from a bookstore in a nearby town. The tablets were a nickel each and the pencils a penny. The Big Chief tablet was most popular with a drawing of an Indian Chief on a red cover with very rough-grade paper on the inside. Flour and water were mixed together to form the paste that we frequently used for artwork and special projects.

The texts were well used, but did not have marks or other signs of abuse. Only actual textbooks were available for student use, and just one was available for each class. They were from a mix of publishers including the "Wooster Reader" from Crane and Co. of Topeka, Kansas and the Board of Education "Kansas Reader." When more than one student was in a grade, they would share the texts. We had no dictionaries or general reading books. The teacher would occasionally bring one of her own personal books to read out loud to the whole school.

Discipline centered on the absolute authority of the teacher. Her word was law. For many students who encountered a problem at school, which was the fault of the pupil, they could expect to get at least as severe a penalty when they got home. My sister and I had no misunderstanding on this point! I only recall the use of a dunce cap one time. Another time a student held his nose against the blackboard within a drawn circle, but I think it was as much his doing as that of the teacher. Whispering was not allowed, and penalties generally required reduced recess time or shortened noon lunch periods.

NOTES.—This blank is for the use of school-district clerks of school districts in which only ONE TEACHER is employed in each district. This report must be made in duplicate—one copy retained by the district clerk and the other forwarded to the county superintendent immediately after June 30. The county superintendent is instructed NOT TO APPORTION SCHOOL MONEY to districts whose reports have not been made out and transmitted, as required by law. If school is a JOINT DISTRICT, the word "joint" should be written before the word "district."

GEO. L. McLENNY, State Superintendent.
C. W. BROOKS.

ANNUAL REPORT of School-District Clerk of _Stony Ridge_

School District No. _79_, County of _Lyon_, Kansas,

for the year ending June 30, 194_5_. Made under official oath, and transmitted to the County Superintendent,

this _Aug 20th_ day of _August_ 1945.

(Signed) _Mrs Edw J Jones_

Clerk of _Stony Ridge_ District No. _79_

SEND TO
COUNTY SUPERINTENDENT
JULY 1

Lyon County, Kansas.

	Males		Females		Total
	White	Colored	White	Colored	
1. Number of persons over the age of five and under the age of twenty-one years residing in district June 30, 194_. (See school census recently taken with each blank sworn to by parent or guardian.)	11		4		15

	First		Second		Third		Fourth		Fifth		Sixth		Seventh		Eighth		Total
	M	F	M	F	M	F	M	F	M	F	M	F	M	F	M	F	
2. Number of different pupils enrolled in each grade. (See teacher's term report.)		1	1			3			1			1				1	6

	Males		Females		Total
	White	Colored	White	Colored	
3. Number of different pupils enrolled in school this year. (Sex and color). (See teacher's term report enrollment.) (Total must be same as total Number 2)	5		1		6

	Males		Females		Total
	White	Colored	White	Colored	
4. Total number days attendance (See teacher's term report)	641½		145		786½

	Males		Females		Total
	White	Colored	White	Colored	
5. Average daily attendance for year (total days attendance line 4 divided by number of days actually taught as shown by line 6) (carry to one decimal only)	4		9		4.9

6. Length of term in days actually taught _160_ in weeks _32_; in months _8_.

7. Number of pupils enrolled who reside in other districts. Male ___ Female ___

8. Teacher—Male ___ Female ___

9. Number of schoolhouses ___ Number of rooms ___ Number of volumes in library ___

10. Number of volumes purchased _6_ and cost of books purchased during the year ending June 30, 194_5_, $ _7.08_

11. Value of school property { Land and buildings, $ ___ { Furniture and apparatus, $ ___

12. Number of schoolhouses built in the year ending June 30, 194_ ___ cost of same, $ ___

13. Amount for which schoolhouse is insured, $ _950.00_

Amount paid for insuring schoolhouse, $ _32.50_

Date of expiration of insurance, _Jan 3, 1947_

14. Amount received from insurance companies for losses, $ ___

15. Is the state series of textbooks used in your district? _yes_

16. Mills levied ___ { General ___ (Taken from rate card of last year; see county clerk.) { Bond ___

17. Assessed valuation of district ___ { Tangible ___ (Taken from county clerk's record November 1, 194_, last year) { Intangible ___

18. Bonded indebtedness July 1, 194_, last year ___ $ ___

Amount of bonds paid for the year ending June 30, 194_, this year ___ $ ___

Amount of interest paid for the year ending June 30, 194_, this year ___ $ ___

Bonded indebtedness June 30, 194_, this year ___ $ ___

FINANCIAL EXHIBIT

Note.—This report must balance with the treasurer's books

RECEIPTS JULY 1 TO JUNE 30	RECEIPTS	
1. Balance in hands of District Treasurer July 1, 1944 (last year). Include all moneys belonging to district	$ 2 35	13
2. Amount received from County Treasurer, except Barnes aid	1134	87
3. Amount received from sale of schools bonds		
4. Amount received from Barnes Aid		
5. Amount received from tuition		
6. Amount received from other sources		
7. Total amount received during the year for school purposes	$ 1370	00

EXPENDITURES JULY 1 TO JUNE 30	EXPENDITURES	
8. GENERAL CONTROL (Board Records, Clerk's salary, etc.)	$ 11	75
9. INSTRUCTION: Tuition to other districts	$ 882 54	
10. Teachers' salaries (include retirement deduction)		
11. Instructional supplies		
12. Total instruction (Lines 9 to 11)	592	54
13. OPERATION: Janitor's salary and supplies	$	
14. Light, power, fuel and water	31 19	
15. Total operation (Lines 13 and 14)	31	19
16. FIXED CHARGES: (Insurance, rent, surety bond premiums)		
17. AUXILIARY AGENCIES: (Library, health, recreation, etc.)		
18. COST OF PUPIL TRANSPORTATION		
19. MAINTENANCE: (Grounds, buildings, furniture, etc.)		4 20
20. TOTAL OPERATING EXPENSES (Lines 8 to 19)	$ 931	68
21. CAPITAL OUTLAY (New equipment, buildings, major repairs, etc.)		
22. TOTAL EXPENDITURES (Lines 20 and 21)	$ 931	68
23. BALANCE IN HANDS OF DISTRICT TREASURER JUNE 30, 1945 (this year)	434	32
24. TOTAL—Line 22 plus 23 (This amount should equal line 7)	$ 1370	00

Note.—Expenditures cannot be greater than receipts (cash basis law). If permission has been granted by the state tax commission to issue no-fund warrants, line 24 will not equal line 7. If such permission has been granted, please give date of tax commission order

25. AMOUNT OF WARRANTS issued by permission of tax commission. Line 24 less line 25 must equal receipts, line 7. $

26. Bonded indebtedness July 1, 194...., last year. $

Amount of bonds paid for the year ending June 30, 194......, this year.

Amount of interest paid for the year ending June 30, 194...., this year.

Bonded indebtedness June 30, 194...... this year.

DISTRICT CLERK'S REPORT OF OFFICERS ELECTED AND QUALIFIED

County Superintendent:

Dear Sir:—On the ....day of April, 194...... the following persons were duly elected and qualified as officers of ....School District No........ ....County, State of Kansas:

Director........ ....Post office........

Clerk........ ....Post office........

Treasurer........ ....Post office........

Dated this........ ....day of........ ....19......

........District Clerk.

Remarks.—The above returns are required by law to be made to the County Superintendent within two weeks after the election and qualification of said officers, as the clerk's report is not sent to the county superintendent until after July 1. Use form 3 in reporting district officers elected at annual meeting.

NAME OF TEACHER (For year just closed)	Grade of certificate	Weeks employed	Annual salary	Type of certificate held (Normal training or state certificate)

TO COUNTY SUPERINTENDENTS AND SCHOOL-DISTRICT CLERKS

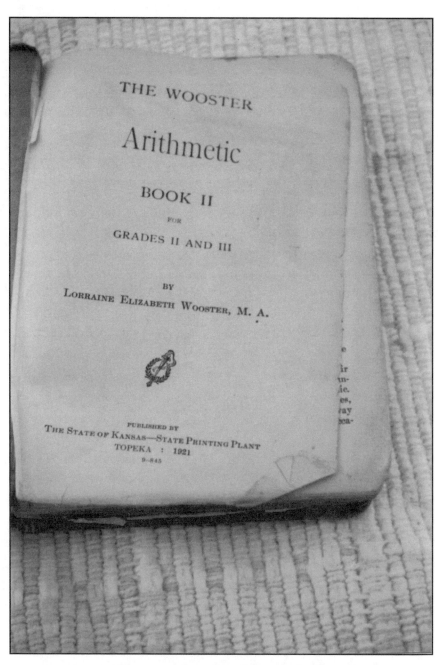

Our second grade arithmetic book.

9

A Typical School Day

Today I start my second reader. Some of the other kids said it is a lot harder than my first one. I wonder if I can do it.

Each student was allowed to learn at an individual pace. When one reader or arithmetic book was mastered, they would move on to the next. None of the students in my schools moved at an exceptionally fast rate and seldom completed more than one year of the curriculum in any given year. The teaching and learning pace was regulated by the teachers and reflected a well-planned program.

On regular occasions, my arithmetic assignment would be to write out the numbers from one to one hundred in my writing tablet. I was instructed to write as close to the left hand margin as possible and shift to the top of the page to continue another column until I had completed the whole assignment. I gradually increased my numbering until the project was finally completed when I reached one thousand — the columns covering several tablet pages. This routine took several minutes each day for several days, and was a convenient assignment for the teacher who used that time to help and direct other students. Some students tried to skip groups of numbers, but the teacher had no difficulty detecting these omissions. Penalties would then be applied and it generally was not tried again.

For other arithmetic lessons, the teacher would write problems on the blackboard. I had a little section of the board that was assigned to me, with my printed name there — and other students had sections as well. I would work these problems out on my tablet, and when completed would raise my hand for the teacher to come over to check them for accuracy. If they were all correct, we would either move to another subject or she would give me instructions on the next arithmetic concept. She sometimes provided a few new problems for me to consider. In grades one and two, our curriculum was reading, numbers, writing or penmanship and spelling. We were allowed to draw very early in first grade. With airplanes flying overhead on a regular basis from the nearby airport, they became the main topic of my drawings. The teacher had a special interest in drawing birds and worked with us throughout the early grades to develop that artistic skill. For projects that required paper that was somewhat transparent, we rubbed lard into tablet paper.

We had little, if any, grammar, history, health or public speaking. The only group activities on a regular basis were singing and spelling. We had no piano in the school, so the teacher had to provide an example of how the songs should sound. The only semblance of a musical instrument was made by placing a small comb covering a strip of paper on our lips to hum a sound. We held contests to determine who could make the most impressive sounds.

During periods of spelling games, all of the students would stand in a line and the teacher would pronounce words appropriate to the age of the student. As might be expected, there would be a little disagreement, on occasion, if it seemed that the younger kids were getting words that might be a bit too easy. If a word were misspelled, the student sat down and watched for the rest of the contest. The last person standing had to spell a final word or the contest would be declared a tie between the last two survivors. I recall no prizes of any kind, but the satisfaction of standing while others were sitting was a lasting one.

Miss Dalton would read to us after lunch each day for about ten or fifteen minutes. The book would generally be an adventure or mystery novel written for kids. It was much like a serial in the movies several years later, where, day by day, we would progress into the story. Every pupil from grade one through eight would listen attentively, and we so looked forward to that time. Our very favorite book was *Black Beauty,* and I remember many days when we could not wait for recess to run out to pet Roger's horse in the stall. No matter what he looked like, he was still our Black Beauty.

Five cents to last for months.

36

♣ 10 ♣

Recesses and Games

It can't be much longer! I know it has to be an emergency to get a drink before we go out to recess, but I will raise my hand and ask Miss Dalton if she doesn't start recess right now. Wait, looks like she's done with Roger. It's recess time!

Although we had no clock on the wall, and no kid had a wrist-watch, we would anticipate with great accuracy when it was recess time. It was certainly not a required break at a given time, but with the teacher working harder than we were, the change was welcomed by all. On days when it was not raining or terribly cold, we would go outside. It was rare that a student would be kept in for bad behavior or because of illness. Misbehavior most often resulted in performing after-school duties before being allowed to go home. If we were well enough to go to school, we were well enough to go out for recess.

Generally, the teacher stayed in during the recess period. This gave her a chance to catch up on paper grading and on finalizing lesson plans for our return. It seems that the separation from the student for a few minutes was also important to her.

We had specific boundaries around the schoolhouse, and seldom, if ever, strayed across them. A moderate size stock pond was located about one hundred yards east of the Stony Ridge School. While it was absolutely off-limits to us, I found out much later that when my mother went to the same school, she and her classmates were allowed to walk there. They would spend recesses and lunch periods near the pond. In the winter, if the ice were thick enough, they could slip and slide across the pond in their school shoes. A wire fence was built partially around it in the winter for our safety. The parents of the students of my time probably knew the trouble we could get into and chose to implement these precautions.

We played all kinds of games outside and rarely were they planned ahead of time. One of the kids would suggest something and off we would go. The regular hide-and-seek game was always popular if we had enough kids to make it fun, and if we could be creative enough to at least hide for a little while without being found. This game was played at picnics and family gatherings all through those early years.

One student would be declared "it," count to a certain number, shout out, "ready or not, here I come," and fan out looking for those hiding. On the school grounds, the only hiding spots were behind and in the outhouses, in the ditch in front of the school, in and around the coal shed and the horse stall, and around the schoolhouse. Sometimes when the grass was tall in the pasture nearby, some of the more adventurous kids would try to hide there. When spotted by the one who was "it," a race would begin to return to the base area or "home." If the hiding student got there first, he or she would be "free." Anyone tagged before getting home safely would be the next "it." The "ally-ally outs in free" cry was the safety signal for all of us who were hiding. It meant that someone else had been caught and we would get to hide again for the next game. I learned many years later that the origin of the cry was, "All the other outs in free." To kids shouting this over and over again, the evolution of the cry seems to make sense.

Another game that was not a favorite of the parents or teachers was Crack-the-Whip. The pupils would hold hands in a long line and, generally, the biggest kid would be the first in line to take off running as fast as possible. With a sudden stop, sideways to the direction of the moving line, the kids of the far end (probably the youngest or littlest) would be thrown from their feet and tumble across the field. We had heard of kids breaking legs and arms and getting other injuries, but nothing serious ever happened in our groups.

When it snowed, apart from the usual excitement of a fresh snow, we had a rare chance of playing Fox and Geese. A large circle was stomped in the snow by the kids and, on occasion, even by the teacher. Several diameters were then tracked across the circle with the intersection of these lines being the lair of the fox. The other kids were the geese and would start the game by running one way around the large circle. If the fox could catch and tag one of the geese, that player would be the next fox. The geese would only be safe back at the center of the circle or running around the circle out of reach of the fox. The main attraction of this game was the chance to be out running and playing in the snow on a school day.

Since recesses only lasted about fifteen minutes, we had very little time to become bored. Although the temptation to throw snowballs was always present, we had a strict rule of no throwing on the school grounds. Once we were walking home, however, we threw snowballs all the way.

One game likely played by every group of one-room school

children in the country had a wide range of rules and names. Basically, the object of the game was to throw some kind of ball over the school house, and either run around to catch it or, when caught by those on the other side, to determine a winner in some manner. The simplest version was for all the players to start on one side of the school and, after the ball was thrown over the roof, run around and find it. The student finding it would then get to toss the ball over to the other side. We called this game "annie-over."

We would divide up into two equal teams, one on each side of the school. After one of the kids would yell "annie-over" and throw the ball over the roof so that it rolled down the other side, they would wait until one of the kids from the other side would catch the ball and run around the building as fast as they could to tag one of the throwing team. The tagged person would then join the other group. The tagging might be by hand or, if the ball was soft, throwing at and hitting the moving target. If the ball were not caught, someone would yell "annie-over" and throw it back over the roof to the other team. The smaller kids sometimes had difficulty getting the ball over the roof. When they determined that it was not going over, they would yell "Pig-tail," and try again. Finally, when recess was over, the team with the most players was declared the winner.

Conversations with others who spent time in rural schools revealed that almost all schools had one version or another of this game. The greatest variation, in fact, might be in the name. Some insist that the full name is "ante, ante, over the shanty" with the ball being the "ante" and the schoolhouse the "shanty." Others called the game "annie, annie, over" and others even used "Andy-over" or "anti-over" in their primary yell.

An outdoor game that attracted the older boys as well as girls was "keepers." The kids would bring marbles from home in little cloth sacks, each player putting a couple of marbles in the center of a large circle drawn in the dirt. Using a larger "shooter," they would try to hit the marbles out of the ring. Whatever marbles were knocked out belonged to the player who knocked them out. The marbles came in all sizes and shapes. Some had special names such as "tiger eyes," "cat eyes" and "aggies." One especially prized marble was handmade of clay and was called a "mib." These were rare and generally were handed down from the parent to the child. Some of my friends had one and knew they would be in trouble if they used it for "keepers." My dad was dead set against this game because he thought it was gambling, and said I had better not even play for the fun of it. I did have a few marbles of the generic type and managed to try my hand at it with a few of the younger kids, but we never played for keeps.

When the weather was too severe to go out during recess, several much more reserved games were played. If the teacher were really enthusiastic, she would lead an activity that would easily last for the whole recess period. Perhaps the game most enjoyed and the most fun had at least a couple different names. We knew the game as either "party line" or "buzz." The teacher would whisper a sentence to a student nearby who would whisper the same sentence to the next student in the row or line. This continued until each student in the room had heard it, with the last student speaking out-loud what the sentence was. Sometimes hilarious variations would result and occasionally complete gibberish was repeated. The creativity of the first sentence was the key to keeping the game going.

We spent many an indoor recess with string games. Generally, two people would play together. Cat's cradle and see-saw were the most popular. It both cases, the younger kids would be taught by the older ones, and they, in turn, would promptly take the game home for the parents or younger siblings to learn.

Winnings.

Playing for keeps.

❧ 11 ❧

Lunches and Snacks

I have only one thing on my mind. As I walk along the road, I think of two slices of white bread with syrup poured over them. We never get syrup in our lunch pail because Mom says it is too sticky and hard to clean up. Maybe if I walk a little faster.

Since we carried lunches every day, sandwiches filled the main course, with occasional roast beef, pork or chicken as an ingredient. We sometimes had lard and salt laid heavily between two slices of bread. They might also be lightly heated on the top of our kitchen stove so that the lard melted into the bread. Jelly and peanut butter sandwiches on homemade bread were a big hit once or twice each week. But fresh vegetables and fruit were quite rare unless it were at the beginning of the school year when the home garden still produced.

Jellies, jams and butters were prepared and canned from a variety of berries and fruits picked in the early fall. These included blueberries, raspberries, strawberries, blackberries, apricots, peaches, gooseberries, apples, blue and white mulberries, pears and grapes. Small purple wild plums, found along the road, were sampled on our walks to school and harvested for plum jelly. On the north side of our house, string woven over and through two fifty-foot rows of fence formed supports for the grape vines. These vines produced several gallons of grapes each year.

Boiled eggs were almost always included in the lunch pail. They were cracked open in any number of ways — including on a classmate's head. Salt and pepper were mixed together into one small glass shaker with a patch of wax paper screwed under the shaker lid to keep it from spilling. Ball or Mason jars served as a safe container for carrying milk, and provided a convenient drinking glass, too. Sometimes these jars were half-pint and sometimes they had a full-pint capacity. The tin lid had a milky-white glass insert under the top for contact with the canned goods and was twisted into place over a red rubber gasket. I remember licking off the smooth glass to get any drops of milk still there after lunch. It seemed that I was always hungry during school days.

For dessert, home-baked cookies were most popular, although occasionally a piece of cake, wrapped in wax paper, was included. We could not trade any part of our lunch with other kids. Lunches were very private, which was typical of Lutheran upbringing.

A large syrup or lard can generally served as a lunch pail. Even little kids carried them. It was funny to occasionally see a first grader carrying a half or even a whole gallon lunch-pail down the road. With this kind of burden, there were frequent, but very short, stops to change hands along the way. These lunch pails were often difficult to open — although all the boys carried pocketknives and used them to pry off the lid. The teacher also had various tools to help open the pail. One had to be careful to avoid the sharp edges under the rim while reaching in for one's lunch. The sharp edge also made washing a problem, as Mom reminded me on several occasions. Later, after we moved to town, my sister and I got our first real lunch boxes — specially constructed with no sharp edges.

If hunger pangs set in on the way home from school, we would eat anything we had left over from lunch. Most of the time, we had already eaten everything in the lunch pail and had only the salt and pepper shaker left. I remember on several occasions shaking a good sample of salt into my hand and licking it off. That may have been the cause of occasional stomach aches which began to hurt by the time we arrived home.

Once we got home, we had a few minutes before play or chores to find a snack. It generally would be another jelly sandwich or a slab of lard on a piece of bread, sprinkled with salt and, if the stove was burning, warmed up. On rare occasions, when it was very cold outside, Mom would heat up either milk or water and mix it with cocoa and sugar for a nice hot drink.

Cocoa came in metal cans and was unsweetened, so it was a matter of taste and availability as to how much sugar we got with it. The heating of the milk was a very delicate process, and it took time to dissolve the cocoa. If it reached the boiling point it would not taste good and had a very unpleasant odor. We would often escape outside to eat our snack and play or do chores until suppertime.

Panhandlers visited us a number of times and begged for food at the door. These visits coincided with our arrival from school late in the afternoon. We had different names for them, including hobos, gypsies, tramps, Indians and Negroes. Mom always told them to wait outside until she brought a sandwich of some kind of meat or lard.

A neighbor lady told us a story of a hobo who said that he was "sure hungry." The lady gave him a banana and prepared a sandwich of hand-whipped thick cream, sugar and a little strawberry food coloring thickly spread on a slice of bread. The man thanked her, saying, "It was the best thing I ever had."

The lunch pail.

Good to the last drop!

12

Visits to the Dump

I can hear the hum of flies as soon as I get out of the car. As I slip and slide to the other side of a large pile of garbage and trash, I see a heavy, flat piece of iron sticking out of a wooden box. I pull it out and drag it over to Dad. With a big smile on his face, he says, "It's part of an old car spring and I bet it is worth at least a quarter. Good job."

On the rare afternoon when Dad got off work early, a great outing would be a trip to the city dump, a few miles from our house. Before we left, we put a few cardboard boxes in the car. We wanted to find useful items for the home, garage or cellar, and each of us had a poking stick to help pick through the garbage and trash. None of the dumped material was separated by category, so valuable finds might be mixed up with last week's leftovers.

For the most part, we would find old wooden shelves, chairs and other furniture that could be repaired, refinished and made usable. Since World War II was in full swing, we were also on the lookout for old pieces of iron or other metal for the war effort. In addition to looking in the dump, we spent many hours collecting old metal scraps from around the sludge ponds near the oil derricks where Dad worked. When a sizable iron pile was accumulated, along with occasional scraps of rubber tires or tubes, we would load it all onto a handmade trailer to sell at the scrap yard in town.

Dad loved to tell the story of a friend of his who was wounded early in the fighting with Japan. When his wounds were treated, a piece of metal shrapnel was removed from his leg. The ragged piece of metal showed the word *Singer* printed neatly in gold on a black background. Apparently some scrap iron from an old sewing machine was sold to Japan before the war and came back as part of the weapons used against us. This seemed to serve as an inspiration to salvage as much useful material as possible.

Dad once found four twelve-inch matching metal wheels. After several days of planning, he decided to build me a real car, powered by a gasoline engine. The finished product looked very much like the go-cart we know today. After several weeks, the day finally came when I could try it out. We pushed the cart onto the gravel road and were able to get the engine started. Dad had built a stick clutch that engaged the drive belt to a pulley which directly powered one back wheel. A piece of wood served as a backrest and a small iron wheel steered the car. This wheel was attached to a cable on a pivoting front axle and worked well to move the front wheels left or right.

I had invited my friend, Roger, to drive the car with me that afternoon. We had really looked forward to this day! I climbed onto the wood seat and, finally, the car began to move! The excitement was short-lived, however, as the metal wheels provided almost no traction on the gravel; I just sat there with the wheel spinning and almost no forward movement. This came as a surprise to my dad, and he said he would try to find some pieces of tire inner tube to stretch over the wheels to provide better traction. But after a few more minutes of slipping and sliding, the engine faltered and finally stopped. That was the end of the experiment. The engine never ran again. The wheels and other iron parts were eventually sold to the scrap yard, and my visions of racing down the gravel road disappeared.

We had no spare lumber on the farm, so when a good piece or two was found in the dump, we grabbed it. I remember when Dad found a couple of two-by-fours about five feet long. He used those to build a pair of stilts for my sister and me. He nailed two footrests at right angles to the long boards a few feet from the lower end. The footrests were supported with straps of leather — taken from discarded belts found in the dump. With a little help, we placed one foot in the stirrup and stepped up and put the other foot on the second stilt. By hanging on to the upper portion, we began to walk on our own. It took some practice, but we got the hang of it, and walked all over the grounds — with our eyes at about the same height as our parents'. This was a great experience and we felt "pretty big." We eventually moved up to a height of two or three feet, and the stilts became a highlight of our play days.

An iron wheel for my car!

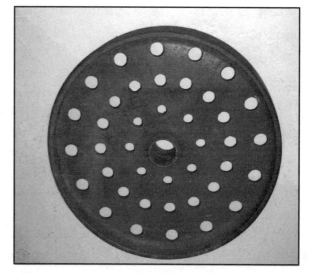

🌿 13 🌿

World War II

How could these faraway people be so mean? They started the war and are shooting and killing American soldiers. I hope Dad doesn't have to go to the war and maybe not come back. I am shivering under my covers. I am so scared.

I turned five years old just a few days before the bombing of Pearl Harbor on December 7, 1941. Although I do not remember the exact day itself, our lives changed dramatically during the following months. War was on everyone's minds and the radios and newspapers persuaded the country to put everything into the war effort. This constant attention concerned everyone. Young kids, especially, had a hard time dealing with it.

I remember going to bed each night with the idea that enemy tanks would crash through our house with soldiers shooting at us. Mom would always reassure my sister and me and, finally, we slept peacefully.

Rationing became a way for acquiring hard-to-get supplies such as gasoline and sugar. We would pick up our ration booklets from various local outlets and Mom would sign for them. Then we headed directly for the grocery store or to a gas station.

The politics of the war started to become real to me when I

heard Dad say that it would be best not to talk German either in public or private. All four of my grandparents were immigrants from Germany and, although they arrived in the 1870s, were singled out and ostracized during the First World War. A number of my granddad's fellow German immigrants had their barns burned down — along with other injustices — during those World War One years. My dad carried with him a very noticeable German accent all of his life, and seemed alternately ashamed and proud of it. From the very beginning, it was made clear that he would seldom talk in his native tongue around my sister or me. The only exception was when we were visited — or were visiting his or my mother's relatives — and they spoke pretty much out of earshot of the kids. I just loved to hear them talk and would sneak close by to get a chance to hear the exotic-sounding words. It was also possible to hear them through the kitchen ceiling into our upstairs bedroom. They seemed so relaxed in their visits, though it took many years for me to get a feel of speaking a foreign language in everyday life. I knew very little German as a youngster, but I was required to become proficient in it as one of my doctoral requirements many years later. I studied German very hard, and many times wished Dad had not been so strict in limiting its use around the house. Nevertheless, I was proud to have learned at least a minimal vocabulary and to have met the language requirement with German as one of my doctoral "tools."

The war also influenced toys and clothes that the kids received for birthdays and Christmas. Specifically, the boys requested some kind of gun, even though these "guns" were simply wood cutouts painted green. No metal toys were available during the war years. Many of the wooden guns were designed to shoot rubber bands which provided a little reality for our "wars." I did not get a gun, but some of my classmates did and brought them to school. An aviator's hat had a little more value, with goggles and a tie strap under the chin. They were made of a thin brown material offering almost no protection from the elements, yet were highly prized. I did receive a hat, but the goggles cost too much.

It was not uncommon for boys and girls to wear scarves as a part of their attempt to keep warm during walks to and from school. As a result of their popularity, aviator scarves were sought after, and just about any material could pass for this very special accessory. On arriving at school, many a small kid would be greeted with special attention if an aviator hat, goggles and scarf were included in his dress for the day.

Because we had so few kids in attendance, we could not deploy many "soldiers" to play war games — especially since the girls had other things to do.

Even in those years, cowboys and Indians was a more popular game. It was just a matter of choosing one or the other and then arguing whether one "shot" the other first.

As part of the war effort, schools across the nation were centers for preparation of bandages. People living in the area dropped off sheets and clothes at the school to be torn into long strands and packaged by the kids. If we did not complete the job at school, we would often take some of the material home to tear, roll and package. In this day of rigorous sterilization, it is hard to imagine that these bandages would have been much help being put together under those old farm conditions. But, we prepared hundreds of rolls and donated them to the local Red Cross. I have often wondered where, or whether, these homemade bandages were used during and after the war. I once heard that most of them were kept in the States in case of an enemy invasion.

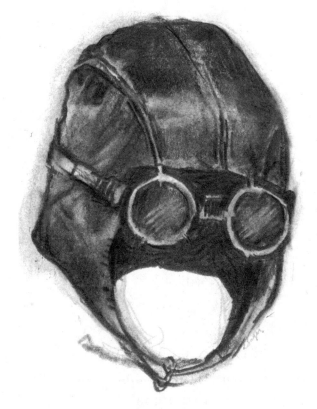

Aviator's hat.

❧ 14 ❧

Airplanes and Parachutes

What a beautiful sight! All those airplanes flying together fill the sky like a flock of birds. When I get big, I am going to be a pilot in an airplane just like the ones flying overhead. I wonder if Mom and Dad and my sister will want to ride with me.

With World War II well underway, we had lots of activity in the skies over our home north of Winfield, Kansas. A nearby airport had been converted to provide instruction to new military pilots. They used small single-engine airplanes like the most popular Piper Cubs. As I stood in our yard, I could hear an almost constant drone of engines overhead and see all kinds of spectacular maneuvering. Later, when I took instructions to become a private pilot, I learned that the WW II military pilots were practicing stalls, short barrel turns, and "touch and goes." For a little kid on the ground, this beautiful sight provided hours and hours of observation and enjoyment.

On several clear, sunny days, the sky seemed filled with parachutists being dropped by slow, low-flying aircraft. The landing target was near the airfield a few miles away, and it appeared that the paratroopers landed near the site. They dropped close enough, at times, to see fairly detailed outlines of their uniforms and backpacks.

From the first view of these beautiful airplanes, I knew that someday I also had to fly. I found all kinds of scrap-wood pieces and cardboard boxes to use for building my own plane. I kept asking Dad for an engine, but he humored me by encouraging me to keep building until an engine became necessary. Of course, that never happened, but it did give me incentive to keep up the exciting work.

Many of the radio shows that were designed for kids during this time featured special promotions relating to the war. Among these was an offer to send in a number of cereal box tops to get an actual Piper Cub control panel with stick controls. I saved and saved until finally I had enough box tops to send. One of the most memorable days of my life occurred when the package arrived. It was much smaller than I expected. But when I opened it and unfolded the sheets of cardboard, there, indeed, was a round paper tube to act as the control stick — along with a two-foot piece of cardboard connecting to a drawing of the control panel of the airplane. Sitting behind the contraption, with a little imagination, I dreamed of flying a real airplane someday.

My dream eventually came true on January 22, 1964, when I took my first solo flight in a Cessna 150 single-engine airplane over my hometown of Emporia, Kansas.

When passing over my parents' place, I tipped my wings to them with enormous satisfaction. My flight instructor had told me to feel free to fly anywhere I wished during the hour-long flight, so I then flew southwest for several miles until I spotted Stony Ridge School. I tipped my wings to that little one-room school, as well, and finally realized my goal set some twenty years earlier.

Piper Cub "J-3" Trainer.
WWII military pilots received their initial flight training in these airplanes.

❧ 15 ❧

Our Victory Garden

Late this spring evening, Dad and I stretch a string around the ground for our new garden. He pounds a wooden stake at each corner and I follow along unrolling the ball of string. Tomorrow, when I get up, the first thing I will do is to look out to see if the neighbor is out there with his two horses. Then I will watch as he plows the ground where we put the strings. An exciting day ahead!

From my earliest memory, I can still see Mom and Dad working side by side in one of our many home gardens. During World War II, the government and community leaders proposed that everyone who could possibly tend a garden do so to assist the national defense effort.

At the first sign of spring, my dad would either plow up our garden plot or hire it to be done by a friend or neighbor. While generally done with a small tractor, a horse-drawn plow was sometimes used. Once the ground was turned over, the odor of the fresh dirt carried for a great distance. The aroma of fresh earth pleasantly surprised me and, along with the explosion of happy cries from the hundreds of birds in nearby trees, signaled the coming of warm, favorable weather.

Once the ground was plowed and had been left for a few days,

Mom and Dad would bring out their garden tools and gently work the ground into a smooth surface that today would remind one of a level golf green. Stakes placed a few feet apart at either end of the plot had strings tied between them. Then, using a hoe, a long V-shaped furrow would be carved into the dirt on one side of each string. This provided an amazing view when the stakes and strings were removed and the plants started to grow up through the ground in magnificent, straight rows.

When we grew big enough, my sister and I would help to sow the seeds within the rows. We just placed an even line of those fine seeds in the bottom of the row when planting carrots, radishes, lettuce, spinach and cucumbers. We had to place the seeds one by one in the row when planting other vegetables such as beans, peas, beets, onions, corn, turnips and cabbage. This quickly became boring to us kids, but our parents would soon compliment us for our "good work" and help us finish the job.

I often wondered how my parents could spend the whole day at hard physical labor and then, after chores and dinner, go out to the garden plot and continue to work until it was totally dark. It seemed that naming these sites "Victory Gardens" gave credence to our normal, everyday duties; yet our work and sacrifice was certainly a subject of national pride!

In addition to gardening, we tried to help the war effort in other ways. Besides collecting scrap iron, Mom saved used grease from the kitchen and poured it into various-sized cans to sell in town. I remember how ugly the dried grease looked, and Mom always tried to sell it before it became rancid. We had very few extra paper-goods on the farm, and not until we moved to town did we become heavily involved in paper collecting for the war effort. The children were pulled into those most stringent war times, and many of us still have vivid memories of it. What the adults lived through is considered exceptional — even in our current time!

Our tools were always sharp.

16

The Pueblo Indians

If I get my work done, maybe the teacher will let us work on the pueblo. I see Mary on the far side of the room. It would sure be nice to sit next to her for the rest of the day.

Apart from the regular three R's of our daily schoolwork, we were occasionally directed to a special project of one kind or another. We worked on these projects during short periods at the end of the school day — and then only if all other work was satisfactorily completed. Generally, all grade levels would work together with each student assigned a specific job. After studying several North American Indian tribes, we decided to build a scale model of a pueblo — the living quarters of the Pueblo Indian. We learned that the tribe used dried clay blocks or bricks to build the walls and then cemented them together by wetting the surfaces with soft clay when the bricks were laid in place. These structures measured a few stories in height and had wooden ladders that provided access to climb from one floor to another.

The side of the ditch in front of the school exposed a very fine clay — quite suitable for modeling. We gathered several hands full of clay and began to build tiny domino size blocks to use for building the walls of the pueblo. We even mixed in strands of hay and straw, as the Indians did, to make the bricks stronger. As the days went by, we brought in different wooden forms in which to squeeze the clay before it dried. Some of the parents assisted in constructing these little rectangles. We also brought in leather laces from old shoes to tie small sticks for the ladders.

My heroes at Sunnyside were the two eighth-grade kids. The girl, Mary, would have to be counted as my first "girl friend." For her to even look at me was an exciting experience! During the Pueblo Indian project, the teacher assigned partners to work together. Mary was my partner, giving me an opportunity to share several hours with her. During the latter part of that year, I calculated when Mary would walk in or out the door from recess — or even at the end of the day. I would run up and, as casually as I could, walk with her a few steps trying to touch her with my shoulder. She never seemed to notice — but I sure did!

Once the Pueblo structure was completed, we extended our study to include native clothes and tools for planting and hunting. We made bows and arrows out of string and tree limbs. In this we had little or no help from our parents; the danger these weapons might pose was a probable reason for their lack of enthusiasm.

This project extended over several weeks, creating some great memories. It demonstrated a fine group effort of all five or six kids in the school, and the teacher seemed to really enjoy our enthusiasm and interest. The particular emphasis on just one tribe of the American Indian left me with a lifelong respect and admiration for their life and time. I noticed that several local creeks and other geographical features had Indian names. When I later studied Kansas history, this early initiation into the Indian culture was of great personal value.

Pueblo Indian home.

❧ 17 ❧

The Pump Handle

—————————————————————————————

As I walk into the room, the teacher tells me that it is my turn to pump water for the washbasin. I quickly put on my mittens and head out the door. I am not about to get my hands stuck on that cold pump handle!

We spent a significant amount of time around the water well or cistern during the school day. Pumping water into a bucket for drinking and hand-washing — or just getting a drink during recess — required permission from the teacher. One kid would pump the handle while other kids drank out of their hands, then another took his or her turn pumping the handle.

The new kids heard every year about the very painful practice of placing one's tongue on a freezing pump handle. For some strange reason, many students found it almost impossible to resist. After touching the handle with his or her tongue, the student became immediately stuck and would generally let out a yell of fright. If the teacher were alerted, she would try to pour warm or cold water over the contact area and ask the student to try to gently remove the tongue. If the experimenter were patient, he or she might possibly escape with little damage. It could seldom be removed easily and a strip of tongue skin invariably remained on the handle. Students would notice this white strip, sometimes lasting for days! After placing the tip of my tongue on the cold handle, I remember trying for a quick getaway without the teacher's help. It brought tears to my eyes, and the pain is a memory that has lasted forever. Rarely did the victim escape some sort of discipline. Most often, it was just a matter of a missed recess or two, but I do not remember a kid trying that trick more than once. Parents were, of course, aware of the escapade because of the kid's discomfort at home. But little help would or could be provided. It just took time to heal.

In my adult years, I spent a good amount of time on the ski slopes of Wyoming and Montana. I have seen a number of kids putting their tongues on the metal bars of the chair lifts and suffer the same fate as we did with the pump handle, but with no teacher to help out. With few pump handles available today, it appears that any cold metal pipe will do, and some kids still have that unexplainable urge to give it a try.

A really cold pump handle.

18

Measles, Asthma and Chicken Pox

I awaken and I can't breathe. Maybe if I turn over on my side. That doesn't help, either. I can't get my breath and loud noises are coming from my mouth. I feel so weak. It is very dark and cold in my room as I sit up and yell as loudly as I can, "Mom, Mom, I can't breathe!" Then I collapse back on the pillow.

A number of diseases were shared by the kids during my first three years of elementary school. When one kid got a cold, the flu, chicken pox or the more serious communicable illnesses such as measles, mumps or whooping cough, others would soon catch it as well. Normally, attendance was good in the early days of fall, but with the first cold snap things changed quickly. There were times when only half of the students, or less, attended classes. The teacher, nevertheless, kept the same routine. One benefit from this, at least, was that more attention came to those who attended.

The first sign of measles or chicken pox appeared as a few red spots on the stomach. Mom checked for this on my sister and me, as it seemed inevitable that we would be in line for the disease. It was rather exciting when they first appeared, because we, too, would miss school. This excitement did not last long, however, as the itching began and little could be done except to apply calamine lotion or sometimes just a cool alcohol swabbing.

With measles, the first part of the treatment required isolation in a dark room until the spots had all "broken out." Our quarantined bedroom soon had a very unpleasant odor. We did not present a very happy sight for my mother or father. I remember the fear in my dad's eyes when he visited us for a few minutes, but Mom always had a way of calming the situation.

We could tell when the measles or the chicken pox began to abate because the spots would start to disappear. The boils and eruptions slowly disappeared from our hairline and forehead. Then they gradually faded from our neck downward around our shoulders, then stomach and finally thighs and calves to our feet. The saying was that they were "falling off our body." Recuperation included taking care of the leftover scabs from the various spots over the body and gradually getting enough energy back to return to school.

I had other occasional problems when I broke out with hives. I was taken to the emergency room at the hospital in town after one especially serious outbreak, and was actually admitted for a few hours during the middle of the day. By late afternoon, the doctor agreed to my going home and coming back in a few weeks for a series of tests. The tests, which included a whole series of scratches up and down my spine and on inner arms, were inconclusive. After that episode I never had another serious outbreak. This was the only time in my life, through my sixty-seventh year, that I was a patient in a hospital.

It took a few years of working on the farm in crop and animal dust to gradually have more and more difficulty with breathing. Finally one late winter evening, I was in some serious trouble. It had snowed all day so my parents carried me downstairs to a bed near the wood stove in the front room. They managed to call our doctor in town and to describe my plight. The doctor said that he would travel the fifteen miles to take a look at me. I looked from a window toward the west where the main road was about a half-mile from our driveway lane. As the hours went by, I watched out the window for his headlights. Finally, through the snow, I saw the lights bouncing along the road and knew the doc had arrived. Mom and Dad were relieved, but nervous, as he came in and walked into my room. After taking my temperature and pulse and checking my chest with the stethoscope, he said that I had survived the worst of the asthma attack and that, by morning, I should be much better. He then visited and talked about general things, including the weather and the possibility of good crops in the spring. My mother gave him a couple of packages of pork chops, as payment-in-kind, and he was on his way back to town. The image of his car driving through the snow is one I shall never forget. His strength and confidence were, by themselves, healing. I was much better the next day and was able to survive several more attacks — until about age fourteen, when other measures were required.

Arriving back to school after a sick leave was almost as exciting as the first day of school. I am sure the teacher felt that with about 20 percent of her class back she could resume a more normal daily schedule. We would have to pick up where we left off before our illness, and put on just a little more pressure to catch up.

Other illnesses such as impetigo or pink eye were never serious enough to miss school for more than a day or two. Lice was a problem that we all had at one time or another. We would get tar soap from the store and, after washing thoroughly, the visible lice eggs, called nits, were carefully removed by hand. Nit picking was a lengthy job lasting several days, and everyone but Dad had to help. Ringworm was very prominent, as well, and its treatment prescribed a daily soaking in kerosene — before and after school, two or three times a day. All in all, my sister and I missed very few days during our rural school experience.

Ford Model A.

"The Doctor's on his way."

19

Holiday Anticipation

Mom just got home from a trip to Olpe to sell eggs. One of her customers had an extra Montgomery Ward catalog and she brought it home for the family to see. Now the old catalog can be used in the outhouse. My sister and I skip to the toy section in the new catalog and find all kinds of things that we hope Santa will bring us. The Christmas spirit is with us!

The anticipation of various holidays throughout the year received special attention by both teacher and students and provided exciting times. Halloween was the first real event to allow us to deviate from the normal routine. This was not a time to get away from regular activities, but the drawing and story-session class time was filled with ghosts, bats, pumpkins and witches.

Since the farm families lived far apart, we had not even heard of trick or treat. By the first of October, though, we had already begun to prepare all kinds of bright orange and black drawings for display in the school. We had no multi-colored construction paper, so we produced the varied images with creative coloring from our crayon boxes. By pressing extra hard on the black crayons and moistening them with saliva we produced shiny black images of bats and witches. The smell, as well as the appearance, of those intense colored images was very distinctive.

The teacher would occasionally bring a pumpkin to class and supervise carving it into a wonderful jack-o-lantern. This was a special treat, as none of the kids' families grew pumpkins on their farms, and they had to be purchased in town. With a candle for light, the happy face was the center of attention for several days.

The Halloween evening and night rituals among the older, out-of-school and high school kids usually involved the tipping over or displacement of outhouses throughout the countryside. The schoolhouse outhouses were most often targeted because they were not as protected as those near a house. Some adults in the area staked out the rural schools in an attempt to keep the vandalism from occurring. But this was not effective unless they were guarded until sunrise or even later the following morning.

Christmas was by far the favorite holiday for all the kids. Our parents told us stories of "old-time" Christmases where full-stage performances were offered in their one-room schools on the last day of classes before the Christmas break. They included Christmas trees with real candles and lookouts posted near the tree to watch for accidental fires.

With decreasing enrollments in the one-room schools, the church became more centrally located to a larger number of participants. Since neither of my schools held church services, celebration of this season within the schools was concentrated around limited decorations and activities. Drawing and coloring Christmas trees with associated ornaments was the main assignment, and we got pretty good at constructing the classic stair-step image of the green pine tree. If our school had any kind of tree, it would be just a pine branch mounted to a flat board with nails. Silver stars either colored or cut from heavy cardboard and coated with tinfoil — laboriously separated from cigarette packages — was a project of the older kids. Many of those were stored away for use in the classroom from year to year. To my knowledge, no decorations were bought from a downtown store.

Santa Claus and his reindeer did not secularize our holiday spirit in the classroom. This was probably a conscious effort by our parents and teachers to keep religion in our thoughts throughout the season. Although we did not have formal prayers in the classroom, it was always assumed that we were guided by religious teachers.

Returning back to school after the Christmas break was always a let-down. But at least we could look forward to some diversion as both Washington's and Lincoln's birthdays were recognized in the classroom's curriculum. The classic assignment was to cut out profiles of both presidents from white paper and to color the images black and hang them up for display during the month of February. We made attempts to review the life and importance of their contributions as well.

Valentine's day received very little attention. Looking back, it seems likely that it would have been a waste of effort with such widely diverse ages of students. We did learn how to construct various Valentine figures out of paper. By folding a sheet and drawing an object, such as a heart, from the folded line, we could then cut the double thickness; when unfolding, we would have a nice symmetrical image and would then color it. With a choice of a bright red crayon, we produced a valentine heart and displayed it with great pride. Since we were all first or second-generation immigrants, the old country concern with protecting the sexes from each other, especially at a young age, would probably be another reason that valentines were not emphasized as a holiday activity.

Easter, on the other hand, provided a most happy and exciting time for the rural school kids. We had lots to do, not only from a religious point of view, but also with Easter baskets and bunny rabbits. Preparing Easter baskets with fresh, soft spring grass, growing on the warm, sunny side of the school, provided an early spring activity and occupied many recesses and project times during this season. We would bring little cans and other containers ranging from very small, such as tobacco cans to larger boxes, to decorate and fill with grasses and cutouts, colored with crayons. Egg coloring was on a very simple scale with dyes made from home products and crayons used to provide different egg patterns.

The last major event of the year was May Day. It excited us because we could prepare tiny paper baskets with hand-made decorations and colorings to place on the doors of neighbors on the first day of May. Each kid had a small number of relatives in the country and in town whom they would honor with a basket. When May 1st came, we would run up to the door of the farm or town house and put the basket on the door knob and run back to the car where Mom would be waiting to hurry off to the next one. Of course, we, in turn, would get our fair share of two or three baskets, and would carry on the old tradition.

The recipients would frequently phone Mom and convey their pleasure in receiving these nice signs of early spring. Mom would then relay these compliments to us and we would fill with pride at our accomplishment.

Portraits of George Washington and Abe Lincoln were featured in most one-room schools.

20

The Sailor Man

As I walk on the gravel road to school, I think of the sailor I am about to meet. Finally, after all these days of waiting, Miss Dalton's friend is going to be with us today, and maybe tomorrow and the next day. I hope he helps me with my spelling.

One morning, during the fall of 1944, Miss Dalton greeted our class with a major announcement. Within the next few days, a sailor would visit us. He was a friend of Miss Dalton's, and they would arrive together at the school. Although he wanted to tell us about his life in the navy, he planned to stay a few days longer to help us with our schoolwork and play with us during recess.

The days before his visit were a most exciting time as we helped to clean up the room and playground. We even drew special pictures to hang up on the walls for him to see. Miss Dalton made certain that we would behave and be kind and courteous at all times during his visit. This special effort sticks very vividly in my mind to this day. She was, no doubt, very intent on impressing him with our class and its discipline.

The kids in the school shared this coming visit with their parents and found a mixed reception. We found out later that some of the parents had wrongly assumed that the learning level might be compromised. Others felt unsure about what kind of disruption an unmarried couple might cause in the classroom.

When the day finally arrived, we filed into the classroom. There he appeared dressed in full white uniform with his hat under one arm and Miss Dalton on the other. Miss Dalton, in turn, put her arm around him. This delightful sight caused us to feel spellbound with this most unusual experience.

We immediately went through our usual opening activities, including the pledge of allegiance, and sang a song or two. We were then introduced to the sailor who told us about his activities in the war. He assured us that the war was far, far away and that the enemy would never reach America. The talk was followed with regular school work which we all attacked with great enthusiasm. The sailor man moved from one desk to another talking with us and helping us with problems. Miss Dalton also worked with us with beaming pride and happiness. Those three or four days went by quickly and were a wonderful experience for all of us. Miss Dalton was supremely happy and smiled the entire time.

When the sailor left, we all assumed routine activity, but shared a little of the sadness exhibited by Miss Dalton. I never heard about her after she later left our school, and I often wonder if she lived happily ever after with that wonderful sailor man.

We all got to wear the sailor man's hat.

21

Home Brew Sizzle

As I get home from school and run into our house, I smell the strong aroma of home brew. I sneak into the pantry, pull back the sheet, and there is the crock pot. If I listen carefully, I can hear a sizzling sound — like Mom frying bacon in the skillet.

If we listened carefully, the sizzle of the home-brew in the pantry would make the little room come alive. Making beer was an annual event in the late fall or early winter, and was legal if it were not sold. After several days of planning, Dad would put a few gallons of malt, along with yeast, sugar and water into a ten-gallon stoneware crock covered with a cotton cloth. The more sugar added, the more alcohol it produced, and the resulting beer would be very "strong." A small light bulb hung directly over the crock to add warmth to the process. After a few days the sweet aroma would drift throughout the house, and everyone, including visitors, would know that beer was brewing. Kids were instructed not to disturb the brew as it had to "work" quietly. We were not supposed to talk about home brew outside our home, but kids at school would share stories about their parents having a "batch" underway. This exciting topic was fun to talk about, and it made us feel really grown up.

Mom or Dad would carefully check the crock every few days and skim a few cups of waste foam from the top of the mix and discard it. To test its readiness, a sample would be tasted using a tablespoon. On rare occasions, Dad declared that the process had not gone well. After testing the brew for several days, he might even decide it was a failure. I remember the great disappointment when the batch was too "green" and had to be thrown out. If the brew were bottled too soon, the bottles would explode and create a mess on the shelves and in the pantry.

Usually, after a few weeks, the brew was ready. About eighty or more brown beer bottles saved from the previous brewing would be sterilized using a bristle brush with soap and boiling water. Then the bottles were placed on cloth towels to dry. Bright gold or silver-colored bottle caps from the grocery store were stacked nearby. The warm amber liquid was then funneled into the bottles and, with an assembly line of Mom and Dad and sometimes an uncle, capped with a hand-powered bottle capper. The full bottles were then lined up proudly in long rows on a pantry shelf. The aging process continued for several days, although a first bottle, or two, needed to be sampled on the same night of the brewing. Although kids were prohibited from drinking alcohol of any kind, we were given a sip of the warm first-day beer as part of the ceremony. I can still remember the tangy taste and especially the smell, which was much more concentrated than it had been during the days leading up to the bottling.

Several days or weeks would pass before the next bottles would be opened. Then it seemed that they disappeared rather quickly. Occasionally, a special guest at our house would be served a bottle, but Dad and Mom drank most of the supply. Dad always talked about saving at least one bottle until the next year to experiment a little and determine if it would get even better over time. To my knowledge, however, that never happened.

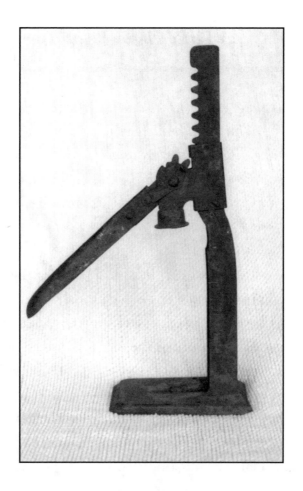

Beer bottle capper.

22

A Little Night Light

It is a very strange experience to come back to school in the evening after already spending a full day here. Mom and Dad are working inside to get things ready for the box supper tonight. Bonnie and I are playing in the fresh, soft spring grass on the south side of the school building. We are making nests for little rabbits. Cars are starting to drive up, so we will soon get to go inside to see all the pretty boxes.

Kerosene lights sometimes illuminated a special evening's activity at the country school. These occasional night events might include box socials, country dances, or a district-wide school meeting. During the early history of the schools, church events might be held in the school buildings. But by the early 1930s, church buildings were erected all over the counties and naturally acted as the new center for these events. Political meetings, however, would be held in individual homes to avoid any shadow of favoritism.

The box social, or box supper, probably provided the most popular night event at the rural school. The entire community looked forward to this money-making activity at least once or twice a year. Proceeds help pay for coal, firewood or repair of the structure; seldom was the money used for supplies or books. I recall only one box supper at Sunnyside and perhaps a couple at

Stony Ridge — but they provided a lasting memory.

Young women who declared their eligibility for marriage prepared decorated box lunches for two. They normally contained homemade pies, breads, sweet and baked potatoes, and beef or pork on rolls, with butter. These fancy boxes were displayed on a large table. After allowing enough time for the male bidders to look them over, the boxes were auctioned to the highest bidder — earning him the right to join the maker of the boxed edibles for supper that night. When he opened the box of his choice, he found the name of his partner inside. Participation in these events not only included students and their families, but many people not directly involved with the school.

If it were determined that one of the boys or young men had a special interest in one of the girls, they would sometimes know which box supper was hers and have every intention of making the high bid. This provided great fun for the other men, as they would bid against the young man, knowing that the price would continue to go up. These prices would most often reach two or three dollars during a time when the daily salary might be only a few dollars. Occasionally, if the box were known to be that of the teacher, the bids would approach twenty dollars.

In addition to these box-socials, a dance would be organized once or twice a year, providing another fund-raising activity. For music, a small organ or piano would be brought in or a local musician or group would perform. The desks were pushed to the sides of the schoolroom and sawdust sprinkled on the floor provided better sliding mobility for the dancers. Round dances, two-step and, on occasion, if a caller could be found, square dancing would be featured. Since baby-sitting was pretty much unknown outside of immediate family, there would be a number of kids in and around the school during the dances. Some of the dances, in fact, appealed to the youngsters who were encouraged to participate. Sometimes adults would dance with the kids to give them an idea of the skill needed and sense of belonging to the group.

Even though the people in attendance would be church-going, peace-abiding citizens, I remember that tempers flared on occasion between young men who tried to gain the attention of the same girl. Liquor also appeared — most often on the school grounds where smoke breaks were held. Although very young at the time, it seemed to me that these evenings ended with more unhappiness than might be expected on such festive occasions.

A pretty Stony Ridge teacher.

23

Antonius Stradivarius

Dad has just removed the fiddle from its black wooden case. He is tuning the strings now. His lips are tight together and his eyes are closed. With his fingers, he is plucking the strings one by one. Then he starts to make little melodies, again with his fingers only. Finally, he places the fiddle on his chest and draws the bow across the strings. What magical sounds!

At the age of nine, my father gave me a prize possession. It was a concert violin brought from Germany by my grandfather. It showed lots of wear from use over the years, but it was absolutely beautiful.

As a young man, my father became quite competent at playing what we today call country and western music. He gained a reputation as a one-man band because he played the accordion, mouth harp, jew's-harp, foot drum, piano, banjo, mandolin, guitar and tuba. His forte, though, was playing the violin, or fiddle, for dances in one-room schools across the flint-hills of Kansas.

He traveled on horseback from his home, located on his dad's farm near the little Kansas town of Bazaar. The violin, in its wooden case, was tied to the saddle horn in front of him. He occasionally told stories of his trips across the open prairie at sunset. After evening chores were completed, he rode for many miles to reach the various schools. He would play for two or three hours and not return home until well after midnight. On a good night, he might earn as much as two dollars — on some evenings he was not paid.

His return rides seemed the most venturous — with the strangeness of full-moon nights to the nearly blind travels of pitch-dark nights. Occasionally he lost his way. He faced flooded streams and unfamiliar markings along the way, which required backtracking. At times, he might not get home until it was time to do morning chores!

He continued to play the various instruments for his own enjoyment during the first several years of my life. He finally concentrated just on the violin. This effort gradually diminished to the rare occasions when he would practice only for a few minutes.

He shared what he knew of the history of the violin when he gave it to me. We had all heard of the famous Stradivarius, and we knew that on the inside of our violin was a sticker that said *Antonius Stradivarius, made in Germany.* Embossed in the wood behind the tuning pegs were the words *Concert Violin* and *Paganini.* I was so proud of this instrument and took lessons from the school music teacher shortly after moving to town in my fourth-grade year. In fact, at the end of that year, I presented a concert to the entire school assembly and played "Twinkle, Twinkle Little Star" — along with a few other short pieces — and received an enthusiastic ovation. Although I was very excited about the response, my recent discovery of baseball precluded my interest in everything else. In fact, a number of times I was diverted from music lessons, while carrying my violin on the handlebars of my bicycle, to a pick-up game of baseball. So ended my music career.

While this was somewhat of a disappointment to my dad, he

was only too happy to see me playing baseball. I put the violin away until I was in my fifties when I decided to have it checked out by experts. I learned that about half of all the immigrants from Germany, in the mid 1800s, carried the same kind of violin — and the inside, eye-catching labels were just a way to sell them.

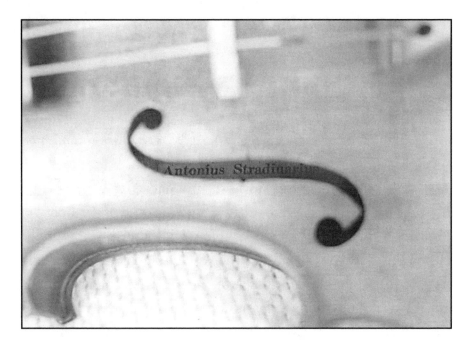

Is it real?

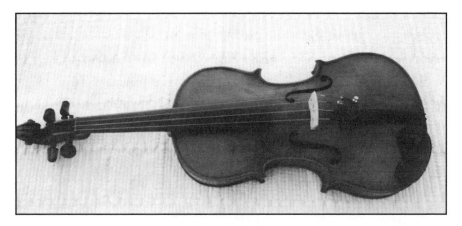

24

The Board of Education

My sister and I watch from a distance as Dad paces back and forth. He will leave for the school board meeting in a few minutes, and he is smoking his cigarette really hard. What a strain this must be!

One of my earliest memories of my dad after work was on evenings when he needed to prepare for a meeting of the Board of Education for Sunnyside School. He would have previously discussed the event for several days and would build it up well beyond its proper setting. He seemed nervous about appearing in public in any capacity, but felt an obligation to serve on what he considered a most valuable governing group. Everyone in the community encouraged him to run for the position. He was nominated and finally accepted, becoming one of three board members.

To prepare for the monthly evening meeting, he arrived home from work as early as possible and washed his hands and face to remove the accumulated oil and grime. He put on a fresh shirt, dress pants — and perhaps the most important of all — his Sunday shoes. This whole process was done with the rest of the family nearby to encourage him.

He was elected treasurer for two consecutive years. Although very little money was involved, he was most concerned with the nature of the accounting and the year-end reports, which would take him weeks to prepare.

One of the many responsibilities of the board members was to help keep the school building well maintained. Occasionally, some of the wood roof shingles needed replacement and windows repaired. The wood flooring was tongue and groove, and wainscoting extended entirely around the room about four feet up from the floor. Since there was no insulation between the interior and outside walls, sharp contrasts in temperature and humidity required cleaning and care on a regular basis. Dad and his fellow board members spent many hours at the school site.

In one instance, Dad and another male member of the board made an attempt to wallpaper the single room of the school. After great deliberation, the materials were finally selected and the big night arrived. Mixing of the wallpaper paste in those days was pretty much an exact science — but at this particular time it was not done correctly. Hanging the large strips of paper on the walls turned out to be a disaster as the paper slipped down the wall about as quickly as it was hung. After several hours of effort, the two went to their homes and talked their wives into helping. They returned, well after midnight, and finished the job successfully.

During the rest of his life, Dad occasionally brought up his experience as a school board member, and seemed pleased with the contributions he made. One of his fellow board members ran for re-election year after year — and finally served over forty years. This service extended well beyond the time when his kids and grandkids attended the school, but he seemed to relish the experience. Dad, on the other hand, seemed to be quite content to follow politics and vote regularly, but was never again actively involved with school-board politics.

Look at all those neat books!

🍂 25 🍂

Meadowlarks and Sunflowers

I carefully open the brand new box of crayons. They look so fresh and smell wonderful. Picking them out, one at a time, they feel good in my fingers. I envision the wonderful year to come, with lots of coloring projects. This really makes school fun!

Art influenced me a great deal during my rural school years. We had only pencils, crayons and a single pair of scissors to help us develop some artistic skill and appreciation. In the first year of school, Mom bought us a six-pack of crayons, but starting in the second grade, we advanced to a full eight crayons. We tried to make the single pack last for the full year. Toward the end of the session, however, few crayons had any paper wrapped around the last inch or so in length.

As the sunflower was the Kansas state flower, and the meadowlark the state bird, both became subjects for many pencil and color drawings. Farmers looked at these two subjects from opposite points of view. The meadowlark had a beautiful song and was so attractive in the early morning and late afternoon when it perched on a fence post silhouetted against the sky. Other birds such as sparrows and blue jays caused constant problems. They lived near the house and stole chicken and cattle feed — and their droppings were everywhere. We never felt sad to see a dead one, and the kids regularly shot them with their BB guns. The meadowlark, on the other hand, lived well away from the house on the prairie, and was a fine and independent example for a state bird.

Sunflowers posed a major problem to the contemporary farmer. Noxious weeds had to be exterminated! Weed sprays were seldom used, and the only way to kill sunflowers was to hoe them down. I do not recall farmers growing sunflowers for profit in those days; likely as not, they would not have heard of sunflower seeds as a food until many years later. Dad often complained that the sunflower was a very poor choice for the state flower.

Sunflowers as art subjects in the classroom were stylized in many ways with their many petals and their large brown center. The sizes of drawings varied tremendously from tiny images of several flowers grouped in patches to a single flower study that filled a full page. Green, yellow and brown crayons found prominent use in sunflower drawing. These three colors, along with black and orange for Halloween and red and white for Christmas, provided a full use from the second-grade crayon box.

After drawing hundreds of line-drawings of meadowlarks and sunflowers during the first few years of school, we knew their natural characteristics by rote. If we ever had an occasion for such a thing as doodling, sunflowers and meadowlarks became the center dominance in such sketches. We certainly could not draw such bizarre things as lightning bolts, swastikas, devils or other subjects! If these images were discovered by the teacher, some kind of administrative discipline quickly followed — and their parents promptly notified! Under no circumstances could the students write on their hands or bodies.

Kansas meadowlark.

❦ 26 ❦

A Last Day of School

It seems like school lasts forever. But now, as I walk to school, I realize that this is the last day of my first grade. Miss Dalton told us yesterday that we were all going to pass, so next year I'll be in second grade!

After nearly a full year at Sunnyside School, we began in early April to plan for the last day of class. The two eighth-graders studied hard for their final exams so they could graduate and attend high school next fall. Day-to-day activities for the rest of the students continued normally. Special springtime projects associated with Easter, May Day, and Memorial Day occupied some of our time, but we also had considerable academic obligations to finish.

Toward the end of the school year, most of us tried very hard to complete the standard curriculum for our grade level. We hoped to convince the teacher to give us at least a peek at next year's requirements. We rarely had a student in school at the next grade level above ours, so this information often surprised and excited us. I think that the teachers anticipated this and gave us their best preview of the next year.

When spring arrived, new plants began to grow around the south and east of the school. Wild Easter lilies and blue Johnnyjump-ups were the first delicate flowers to color the meadows. The teacher took advantage of these warm days by extending our recesses a few minutes. She also provided a few projects that allowed us to be outside — even during "company time." These experiences will always be remembered. Along with the lilies and jump-ups, we picked daisies, dandelions and other species to make most colorful and sweet displays to take home — and to show off with great pride on the kitchen table.

Efforts were made in some schools to provide various contests with other schools in the region. These included foot races of all kinds and baseball throws. Large schools sponsored team competitions between their regular athletic teams and student pick-up teams. Spelling, speech and drama contests were included, in addition to many other activities. In my schools, however, we did not compete with any other schools during my rural school experience — probably due to very small enrollments and limited financial support. With so few kids, some of the parents joined us as we played baseball workup and horseshoes.

We were so relieved to hear that the eighth graders had passed their exams and would attend high school in the fall. By tradition, parents and friends were invited by word-of-mouth to attend last-day activities. This day included recognition of the graduates and a potluck dinner. When the day finally arrived, the morning lasted forever while the teacher did what she could to hold the kids' attention. People would start arriving about mid-morning with food and table settings to prepare for the luncheon. It seemed that the entire community had arrived by noontime, so we were dismissed to our parents. We then had lunch and were allowed to play in the schoolyard for several minutes before the ceremonies began.

Finally, the teacher introduced the graduates who were dressed in their best Sunday clothes. I was a little sad to think that this may be the last time I would see Mary. Everyone was so proud of the graduates' accomplishments, and several short speeches were presented on their behalf. The school year concluded when each eighth grader presented an original poem or an essay, especially written for this occasion. I really felt proud to be a part of all this. What could have been more inspirational than to receive this wonderful send-off into the beautiful summer?!

One baseball glove for the whole school.

27

Tornado Alley

It is a very warm and quiet afternoon. Mom, Bonnie and I are in the storm cellar getting boxes ready to carry outside to the moving truck. Dad walks up to the cellar door and yells, "Let's leave the rest of the stuff down there! I don't like the looks of the sky!" This could be another night we spend in the cellar!

When we first moved to the oil lease in 1942, preparation for defense against a tornado took high priority. Tornadoes concerned everyone who lived in this part of Kansas! Several tornados would strike the area each year — usually from April through August. Just a few days after we moved in, Mom and Dad determined a location to dig a storm cave some yards to the east of our new house.

Once the site was staked out, the pick and shovel work begun. Since Dad worked almost around the clock at his own job in the oil fields, he could only help on occasion. Mom did most of the digging, the first part of the job accomplished with just a shovel. It didn't take long, however, to reach several layers of rock and from that point on, Mom used the pick for hours at a time. When a depth of about seven feet was reached, Dad constructed concrete walls and floor — along with a drain — into a gravel base within the eight-by-ten foot hole. Steps on one end of the cave were constructed of wood, and a six-inch reinforced concrete ceiling was poured over one-by-six inch boards. After almost six months of steady work, the main part of the cave was completed. Finally, the cellar door was constructed and fit into place.

The furnishings of the cave consisted of several potato shelves about six feet long and thirty inches wide. These were used to store vegetables during the fall and winter months. During tornado season, the two bottom shelves were emptied and supplied with several sleeping blankets for Bonnie and me. This left an aisle of about two feet up the middle. My sister and I were carried out to the cellar when an approaching storm appeared. Mom sat on a wooden chair, while at her side an oil-burning lamp provided our only light. Dad took his place on the steps leading out of the cellar. When the storm subsided, Dad would peek out and declare the storm had passed. We were then carried back into the house to sleep the rest of the night.

On our last day on the lease, two hired men loaded our furniture to help move us to my grandfather's house. As the men packed the last things into the truck, the air suddenly became very quiet. Severe weather was imminent — a tornado was on the way! A long black cloud with a band of blue sky directly below appeared in the west! We watched for a few minutes, as a tornado dropped into the blue band and roared directly toward us! It surged to the ground, pulled back up about halfway to the dark cloud, and then dropped down again. When it scoured the ground, it pulled up dust and objects large enough to see within the swirling mass.

We all rushed to the storm cellar, even the two movers. Dad lingered at the top of the steps until the last minute, then pulled the door down just as the twister hit! Incredible thunder and lightning, along with high winds, tore through our property for several minutes. Dad held the wildly vibrating wooden door as tightly as he could, even though several latches were fastened from the door to the inside of the stair well. On the ceiling of the cave was a pipe about five inches in diameter intended for ventilation. As the cyclone (as it was then called) went over us, the air was sucked through and out the pipe. It made a terrible, whining sound. We were all very frightened, and my mom did all she could to soothe our fear. Outside, we heard a deafening noise — almost as if a train locomotive roared over the storm cellar. The tornado ended very quickly, and my dad's calmness gave us courage. When we opened the cellar door and walked up the stairs, we were shocked to see the debris strewn around the grounds: our house was twisted several feet off its foundation, the roof had large, jagged, three-to-four foot holes blown out. I remember that the yellow house looked very much disturbed and in a kind of "slouch" as the tornado disappeared to the northeast. We had opened the windows of the house just before we went into the cave as we had been instructed so many times. This probably saved the main structure of the house — as varying pressures did not affect the main living area, but offered no protection to the closed attic area.

After picking up as much of the debris as we could, we saw the moving truck leave yet that night. Our family piled into the old family car, and by midnight we traveled to our new home, some 100 miles to the north.

Here it comes!

28

The Move to Stony Ridge: Back in Time

It is early morning and I look around my new bedroom for the first time. In the middle of the room a big black stovepipe comes up right through the floor and out the ceiling. Mom says that the pipe will help us keep warm next winter. Bonnie is sleeping on the other side of the room. I really have to go to the bathroom. Should I use the bucket under the bed or get dressed and run to the outside toilet?

In the early spring of 1944 Uncle Carl and Aunt Clara visited us one weekend on the Diechman lease and asked us to move to the fully operational home farm near Olpe, Kansas. They wanted us to help Grandfather Schroeder run the farm. Uncle Carl and Aunt Clara had helped him for a number of years, but were buying their own farm a few miles away. Almost physically broken from the work on the lease, my dad and mom decided that this would be a welcome move. Dad heard rumors that he might be drafted into the service, and he guessed he might be part of the proposed invasion of Japan sometime during the next year. By moving, Mom, my sister and I would at least have a place to live in his absence, and the farm would help to support us.

What a shock it was! The old home place was a far cry from the house near Winfield. It was as if we traveled back in time. For starters, we had no electricity and no indoor plumbing. Water was pumped up from a windmill down by the creek, and had to be stored in case the wind was not blowing on a day when we needed it. An outhouse sat fifty feet north of the house, and portable pots or buckets were located under every bed for nighttime needs. The outhouse, or privie, was built of wood and placed over a hole dug in the ground. Holes cut into the board indicated where people would sit. Outhouses were described by the number of holes cut into the bench, such as "one-holers or two-holers." The size of the holes would vary for the larger adults and the smaller children, and it was not unusual for dad and son or mom and daughter to "go" at the same time. About once a week, Dad would sprinkle lime powder into the pit as part of the cleaning process. Finally, when the pit was full, a new hole would be dug and the old one filled in. That would then make a good spot for planting tomatoes and other vegetables.

We didn't have a potato cellar directly under the house on the oil lease. On Grandfather's farm, however, there was one just below the kitchen, accessible through a doorway and down some steps. Within a few days after our arrival, Mom decided to take some things down and, as she stepped on the first wooden step, heard a rattle. On the next step down a two-foot rattlesnake was coiled. She stepped back and ran outside to get a hoe. With one swing the rattlesnake's head was severed! She looped the snake over the hoe and carried it out to the backyard to bury. She returned with a small shovel, found the head and buried it as well. That was a startling preview of a number of encounters with snakes of all kinds.

Sparse furnishings were scattered throughout the first floor of the house. We had a large dining table, but only four chairs. For additional chairs for the table and the rest of the house, we found used nail kegs from the lumberyard in Olpe. Kerosene lamps lighted each room in the evening. We sometimes used candles as a backup, but they were considered too dangerous to use on a regular basis.

In our former home near Winfield, we had a regular metal bathtub and a propane water heater and refrigerator. On the farm, the bathtub was a three-foot-diameter washtub with water heated on the kitchen stove. We all took a bath about once a week, usually on Saturdays. All the members of the family used just one tub of water. Bonnie would take her bath first, and I would jump in right after she got out. Mom added a little hot water and took her bath next. When the weather was not too cold, Dad took his bath in the creek. At other times, he bathed in the tub, with warm water added, after the rest of us had finished. The icebox used ice either collected and stored for a time from our creek during wintertime or delivered weekly by truck from Olpe.

With the addition of my grandfather, called "Pop," the family now grew to five. We immediately began to squeeze out a living directly off our one-hundred-and-twenty-acre farm. There was little waking time spent during the evening hours. It was truly "early to bed and early to rise." In the late summer, we might have an hour or so after chores to just sit on the concrete slab in front of the house or play around on the farm grounds — but the 5 a.m. get-up time was only too regular.

We had two heating stoves — one a cook stove with an overhead compartment, and the other a long, low wood heater in the living room. The stovepipe or "flue" from the living room stove extended upwards through my bedroom on the second story. That was the only heat upstairs, although occasionally we opened a grate on the floor to get heat from the living room below. This was seldom done because it would become too cold downstairs.

On cold winter nights, my sister and I would warm up our pillows by holding them very close to the wood stove until they were so hot they would sometimes have a burning odor. We would then fold them, run upstairs and jump into the cold bed and onto the warm pillow. There were many nights that this trick was about the only way to get us to bed. On many mornings when we awoke, there would be a jarring experience as we found a thin sheet of ice around the pillow and covers from the frozen condensation of our breath during the night. On occasion we found snow on the bed and floor that had blown in around the windows. Because of this cold, we liked to keep our clothes under the covers during the night. They would be warm when we awoke and we would dress while still under the covers. Of course, using the pot under the bed during the night was almost a non-event. Just "hold it" till morning was the cry.

During the night, we often heard mice running in the ceiling of our bedroom. Since we slept on the second floor, we would also hear them underneath us between our floor and the downstairs ceiling. It sounded like they were playing, and many times it sounded like several mice running at one time.

Selling cattle, eggs, corn, wheat, chickens and cream was the primary way for us to make the cash to buy food and supplies not grown on the farm. Although we bought most of the goods ten miles away in Olpe, we occasionally drove to Emporia to get flour and a few other supplies. We brought our own flour sacks that were used over and over until worn too thin to use any longer. Mom then used them to make clothes of all kinds. These were primarily made into dresses for the girls and shirts for the boys.

We were never embarrassed with the flower design when working in the fields or in school.

During that first summer, we drove by the "new" school that my sister and I would attend in the fall. What a desolate-looking building — with high weeds around it, and no sign of a playground — or even a path leading to the road! To make matters worse, we overheard our parents talking about the difficulty in getting a teacher for the fall and the anticipation of a very low enrollment. Some talk centered around possible closure of the school. This would result in at least a four-mile walk to get to the closest school, and would require some kind of transportation other than walking. This was most disturbing to my parents. However, a cousin of mine, Herman, moved in with us in the late summer and would be in the first grade. We three, along with Harold from up the road, provided a sufficient enrollment for the school board to find a teacher, so we started school at Stony Ridge in early September.

Pop.

🐦 29 🐦

Chores

It is very early in the morning and still dark. I wear my heavy coat and am walking, with my bucket, to the milk barn. Dad left the cows in last night, so no one had to bring them from the pasture. It is so cold I can see my breath.

Perhaps the most difficult adjustment my sister and I had to make on our new farm was the expectation that we contribute time and effort to a number of chores. They were within most of our capabilities, but we certainly did not know it at the time. Where we had lots of playtime at our previous home on the oil lease, our time on the farm was nearly filled from sunup to sunset.

We were both assigned the task of walking to the pasture west of the house to herd in the cows for milking. We would milk at about 5:30 in the morning and 5:30 in the evening. The early morning walk to get the cows was right after breakfast. Whatever playtime we might have after getting home from school would be interrupted with the cry, "Time to go get the cows." It was natural to be a little sluggish — especially after just walking a mile and a half from school — but Dad or Mom would give us a quick bit of encouragement with a scolding word or a swat on the bottom. Sometimes the cows were very close and other times nearly three-quarters of a mile away. Once they were "shooed" into the pen near the barn, the real work started.

We generally milked eight to twelve cows. Mom would find herself completely engrossed in preparing supper — and all the other duties of the house — and rarely joined Dad, my sister and me in the milking barn. We scattered hay and other feed in front of the milking stalls for four or five cows at one time. When we opened the door, the waiting cows made a rush for their individual stall and started eating. We then walked along to secure their heads within the stall with a long two-by-four board wedged tightly with another, shorter board.

Our milk stool had just a single leg, and we had to learn to balance ourselves for several minutes at a time. Very young children would start with three legs on the milk stool, but this kind wobbled uncomfortably.

Some of the cows would be quite relaxed and others would be defiant. Several of the cows had to have devices on their back legs to keep them from kicking. These "hobbles" were made of iron and chain and were tightly cinched. This limited the cow's movement and made it difficult to knock over, or step into, the milk bucket or kick the milker. With younger milkers, some cows would still be able to make life miserable. They would bump the bucket over and do whatever else they could to make milking difficult. As a youngster got older and stronger, he or she could hold the bucket between their knees and, with a solid support, resist these blasts. The cows would, on occasion, hump their back and give the milker a few seconds' warning that either a urine or manure release was about to happen. We would duck for cover with the milk bucket in one hand and the milk stool in the other and retreat out of harm's way until the episode was over. Dad did not take to this kindly and would give the cow a firm, swift kick in its lower ribs. This stopped most of them, but some stayed persistent and always made trouble. Eventually, they all would start to become "dry" and only be milked once a day — then finally not milked until the next calving. These would be great days when the tough cows would be "done" for another season.

On cold winter days, and with very cold hands, we found the area between the cow's udder and her hind leg to be very warm. Several minutes were spent warming up our cold bare hands before actually going to work with the milking. Everyone had their own milking pace — with Dad milking three or four cows to my one. I generally milked two each time and my sister milked one. Looking back on these times, one wonders just how clean this milk was before pasteurization became common.

In addition to milking twice a day, my sister and I also had the responsibility of gathering eggs at least once a day. This rather easy task posed two possible problems. Sometimes we would have to lift the hen up from her nest to look for eggs and, if she were cantankerous, we could get a good peck that sometimes drew blood. On one occasion, a chicken ran right up my bare back and badly scratched it. By dinner the next day, that hen was the main course. The other problem would be finding a snake in the nest. If it were a black snake, we simply lifted it out of the nest and took it to another part of the barnyard. They ate rats and mice and were considered friends. If we found another kind of snake in the nest, we reported it to one of our parents who then took care of it.

When we had a little time after chores, we would look for hidden hens' nests. This was a recreation that we had to do on a regular basis, and we had good fun doing it. Many of the hens were concerned with having their own chicks rather than having the eggs "stolen" by the farmer. Our goal was to find a nest of fresh eggs but, on occasion, we arrived too late — and found chirping chicks instead. In other cases, the eggs were deserted and rotten.

After milking each day, some of the whole milk was then hand-fed to needy calves. A rubber nipple was attached to the bottom of a bucket and held over the fence while the calf drank. After a few weeks, the calves would grow to the point where they needed a half-water and half-milk mixture. Finally, they would be totally weaned if we fed them separated skim milk for a few more weeks. Then they started to eat a normal grass and grain diet. Skim milk was also fed to the hogs. After allowing some of it to sour, the "clabber" milk was fed to the chickens. They especially thrived on this curdled food.

The milk separation process was a very labor-intensive project. The hand-cranked separator was a rather large machine. By regulating the speed of the crank, we established a degree of separation with the general goal of recovering as much cream as possible. We separated the milk quickly after milking and it would generally still be warm. We kept a cup near the separator to catch and drink as much of the separated milk as we wished. If one developed a taste for this kind of milk, it was quite tasty and filling. After separation, almost all the cream was contained and sold to the dairy in Olpe. A dairy employee traveled around the county and picked up the filled cream cans at the main road from the house. At other times, we took cream directly to town and sold it. This weekly event provided some ready cash for living expenses.

The separator had to be cleaned after each use. It contained a few dozen cone-shaped metal pieces that varied very slightly in size. They were about six inches in diameter and nested one over the other in an exact pattern — with numbers placed on them to keep them in order. Each was washed separately in lye soap in a large dishpan, rinsed in boiling water from a teakettle, and placed on a towel to dry. The two long spouts coming from the machine also needed cleaning. A bristle brush, designed for that purpose, used lots of soap and hot water to scrub the surfaces. Any chance of contamination had to be eliminated or we would have no pay-day that week.

Not all of the cream was sold in town. We made our own butter by placing thick cream into a lidded half-gallon syrup can. Generally, Mom shook it back and forth for an hour or so until butter formed and thumped within the can. When the lid was opened, the butter would be at the bottom of the can and butter-milk floated on the top. My sister and I were eventually trusted to start the shaking process as we walked throughout the house and around the yard. But, one day, the lid came off in the house and it all spilled to the floor. We were scolded and not allowed in the house again while shaking the butter can.

One chore that all the children looked forward to was burning the pastureland in the early spring. It was considered quite dangerous, but this fact probably added to its magic. We were lectured on our precise duties and were expected to carry them out without fail. Dad would first determine that the wind blew in the proper direction and then hoped to get the job done before any major weather change. During the entire process, the adults always worried about the wind's changing direction.

Dad took a gunnysack soaked in kerosene to the starting line on the prairie. Lighting one end, he quickly ran along for several yards dragging the burning sack behind him. He repeated this several times until he had a long string of burning grass moving down-wind. All the helpers, adult and children alike, had water-soaked gunny sacks to help control the speed and direction of the fire. When a fire break-out would occur — where one area was burning too fast — we beat the area with the wet sacks to put the fire out or to delay it. Sometimes we found ourselves on the burned side of the flames and felt our feet heating up through our shoes. This was a dangerous situation and we were told to jump across the fire-line immediately!

If the burning of the land were not completed by sunset, the lines might be manned all night. With several neighbors also burning during the same time, we often saw the magnificent red night sky in two or three directions from our work site. If our burn were over, we sometimes crossed the creek to the south and climbed up the hill to look at the many winding, burning lines of fire on the neighboring fields. This was truly a highlight for everyone — especially the children. We were ready to do this again next year!

A magnificent prairie fire.

Milk separator.

30

Hitler, Louis and Captain Midnight

Dad just arrived home from selling cream in Olpe. He is almost running as he comes through the kitchen door. "Hitler is going to talk on the radio tonight, and Mr. Brinkman at the hardware store said that we should be able to get it on our radio," Dad shouts. "Let's get the chores done!"

Listening to the radio provided the main entertainment on the Schroeder farm. When Mom was young and living at home, only one radio existed within a several-mile radius. A big multi-family event was to travel to this relative's house and spend the evening listening to various programs. Then and now, the adults and kids sat spellbound and found the evenings to be most enjoyable.

Pop had purchased a large console radio and permitted us to listen to special shows right in our own front room. This room was primarily used for the heating stove, and in addition to stacked wood, it occupied at least half the floor space. The radio was near a window on one wall, and various wooden nail kegs, along with one or two overstuffed lounge chairs, filled the rest of the room and gave us all a place to sit. With no electricity, the large batteries used to power these radios were charged by attachment to either the windmill generator or to a running tractor engine. Disappointment was long and bitter if a battery's power ran down during an evening's radio session. With only candlelight to see by, a flashlight was sometimes used to provide enough light to change the station or to adjust other controls on the radio. Only the head of the house had this privilege, and he took it very seriously. To get better reception, an antenna wire was fed through the window and strung into the window screen. The car battery used to power the radio lay nested on the windowsill of the stone house.

Major Bowes' Amateur Hour and the Arthur Godfrey Show provided our main entertainment attractions from Topeka's WIBW-AM radio station. These programs offered a wide range of entertainment. On very rare occasions, when it rained and we couldn't get into the fields, Dad experimented with the radio and occasionally found a late afternoon kids' show for my sister and me. I heard Captain Midnight a couple of times and really enjoyed it. In fact, I was listening to that program when it was interrupted to announce the death of President Roosevelt. I remember shouting to Mom that the President had died, but she didn't believe me until she also heard it on the radio a few minutes later.

On a couple of rare occasions, a heavyweight-championship boxing match would be broadcast. It caused great excitement across the country. On fight night early chores were completed and we gathered around the console radio. Early moments of the broadcast would include interviews with the fighters — and of special note was the voice of Joe Louis. We were "glued" to the radio, gathering as close as possible to hear what became a very recognizable and loved voice of the "Brown Bomber." Many years later, when I would catch a sentence or phrase by Louis, my mind's eye brought back visualized memories of those distant evenings.

Other historical voices we heard included Adolph Hitler.

During the time the war neared its end, special programs featured him during live broadcasts from Germany. Although spoken in German, these broadcasts were understood by Pop and by my dad, and they translated some of the speeches for us. They always showed a certain respect for him as the leader of their home country, but they expressed patriotic American feelings in the effort to defeat him. On other evenings, we listened to Winston Churchill, "direct from London," with Edward R. Murrow as the American commentator. Of course, whenever President Franklin Roosevelt spoke to the nation, we made every effort to tune in. These broadcasts made a huge impact on our family, and their content helped us plan our future.

Throughout the whole radio listening process, I recall the look on the adult faces as one of complete fascination and awe at what they were experiencing. They wrinkled their brows and gave expressive quick looks at each other. We kids just listened and watched — never speaking.

The old Silvertone.

☙ 31 ☙

Zion Lutheran Church

Another long day in Sunday school. If I sit here quietly, maybe I won't get called on. I have no idea what the teacher is talking about. How do the other kids know all those things? Barbara is answering all the questions again just like always. I can't wait until we get to go outside before church starts.

Sunday school and church on Sunday mornings was a very regular routine. Located about five miles from our farm, the travel distance seemed very long — especially on cold winter mornings. These days required a little earlier chore duties, as we had to return inside to dress in our Sunday best. This routine harbored no resistance from us. Great care and sacrifice was made by all families to make a special commitment to honor God and the church with the best we could produce. This not only related to outward material matters, but deep inside spiritual ones as well. For the adults, their perceived duty provided solid role models of steadfastness and devoted respect for which the church stood.

The kids had to make a major effort to try to comprehend the church services and Sunday school lessons. These lessons were taught by various members of farm families who, many times, had as much difficulty interpreting the gospel as did the youth.

Learning Christian discipline, however, exacted a fear of a parent's wrath — which was enough for most of us to at least pretend to understand and to participate. We had to sit still in little groups assigned according to age. Sunday school lasted almost a full hour — and we had no papers to color or handouts to read! Other than a Bible and a hymnal, the class relied directly on the leadership and teaching ability of the teacher. We listened to children's Bible stories. After they were read to us, the teacher asked specific questions about the stories. Other topics generally centered around the ten commandments and what they meant to us and to the teacher. A creative teacher sometimes made drawings and showed us various pictures from the Biblical stories. As the session concluded, we had just a few minutes before we joined the congregation for the regular church service.

Parents visited with each other during the Sunday school hour, and at church time sang proudly and listened intently to sermons that would last a full half-hour or more. With communion, baptisms and other activities, a service rarely let out in less than an hour and a half. This period tried the patience of even the most well-behaved children. They constantly squirmed around in their seats and, of course, the parents would then forcibly separate misbehaving kids with stern admonitions of what would happen when they got home! No drawing, talking, whispering or any other playful activity was permitted. We just sat still for the hour and hoped to survive. If we didn't do as we were told, we could expect a swift swat from our parents on the way to the car after the church service.

When church was finally over, we filed out and shook the preacher's hand at the door. After a little more visiting, we headed home and found, almost by magic, a dinner of roast beef, potatoes, gravy and vegetables of all kinds. Dessert was always a part of the Sunday feast and consisted of cakes, pies or fruit. The kids had to change clothes before dinner, although the adults sometimes would come to the table in their church clothes.

Of course, we realized after the years went by that Mom got up extra early to prepare the dinner before church. On arriving back home, it would have been cooking in the oven and the wood-burning stove just long enough to serve some of the tastiest meals we ever had.

Zion Lutheran Church.

32

Sunday Afternoons at Pop's

Chores are over and I watch out the west window to look for approaching cars. I see a cloud of dust to the south. It has to be Sonny, Gilbert, Geraldine and Lloyd. Just now another dust cloud appears to the north. That's Larry and Carolyn. Oh, boy! This is going to be a great play-day!

Sunday dinner leftovers were few and far between since visitors showed up in the early afternoon and would help themselves to the remaining food. Our home provided a center for the extended family to get together and, with the exception of holidays, Sunday afternoons provided the favored time. On at least half of the Sundays of the year, most of the families on my mom's side showed up to visit at about the time she got the dinner dishes washed and the table cleaned.

Carefree Sunday afternoons prompted the kids to play in the yard or nearby fields. Since my mother had nine brothers and sisters, all living within easy driving distance, we had so many cousins that natural age groups played together. With girls and boys playing separately, we had as many as five or six distinct bands of kids running around.

Once the relatives had all arrived in the afternoon and gave their regards to Pop, he took a short nap. This was his only nap of the week as he was always up at first light every day and generally worked until dark.

On these Sunday afternoons, my dad would walk out to the shop to sharpen tools. I think he wished to get away from the routine of regular day-to-day chores and work. He occasionally tinkered with various wood projects, as well. As it turned out, Dad was honing his talents for what was to be a lifelong profession as a carpenter and house builder after we left the farm a few years later.

The afternoon activities during the winter ended about four o'clock with most of the people heading home to do chores — while in the summer, people stayed until well after dark.

What a great disappointment for my sister and I — and a cousin or two — when everyone else had to leave! On the other hand, summer evenings were enchanting with cicadas starting to chirp — we called them cady-dids — chickens drifting toward the chicken house to roost for the night, barn swallows diving for bugs, other birds settling in tree tops and a special kind of twilight. Once darkness set in, fireflies and bats would come out by the hundreds. The bats would dive toward the ground from various heights and "buzz" very near us as we played in the yard. They obviously fed on bugs in the air, but we had the idea that they "targeted" us, and flitted this way and that so not to get tangled in our hair. We heard this tale many times, but somehow were fortunate enough to escape this terrible fate. With the birds and chickens finally settling for the night, all kinds of other sounds erupted from animals and insects from our creek nearby, and from howling coyotes in the distance.

Our barn today.

33

Sunday Evenings at Pop's

I'm sitting on Dad's lap watching the men play poker. The pot is getting bigger and bigger, and Dad can't believe that there is so much money in the middle of the table. They finish the game and Dale wins. With a big smile, using both hands, he drags in all the coins. What a beautiful pile of silver!

With Sunday afternoon activities winding down around four o'clock, major changes started about an hour later. The women from the families who stayed for the evening collected the food and dishes from the dining room table and scrubbed it down in preparation for some high-stakes poker. The Schroeder brothers, their in-laws and a few friends and neighbors found a place around the table and began a long evening and night of mostly five-card draw, double ace-in-the-hole, and a few games with "wild cards."

No more than seven men played at any one time, but as many as twelve to fifteen squeezed around the table to watch the action. The ante was a quarter, with a fifty-cent limit, and three raises. No poker chips were used. Coins jingled off the bare table when tossed into the pot — the ringing sound could be heard throughout the house. Each player had a number of dollar bills in front of him with his coins neatly stacked on top.

As part of the preparation for the evening, cases of cold beer were iced in washtubs on the nearby porch. A beer of choice was selected over the weeks, but occasionally a new brand would show up, and everyone had a great time tasting and comparing. The regular players rotated the duty of providing the beer each week with the occasional visitor welcome to "have one on the house." My Uncle Carl was always hungry. On several occasions, as late as midnight, he suggested that we needed some fried chicken. Some of the women then went out to the chicken house, chose a couple of sleeping chickens, and within an hour or so, had fresh fried chicken on the table for all!

My dad and a few others around the table seldom played — but would be invited in for a hand or two. After losing one or two dollars, Dad usually sat out the rest of the evening. He really enjoyed playing, but just didn't have the confidence nor enough money to give it a full try.

This regular weekly game was widely known throughout the area, but a certain nervousness was evident as these games were unlawful at the time. The winning players around the table would often disappear into another room or to their cars for a few minutes to hide their winnings. I often heard that someone always sat at the front-room window and looked to the west for any strange cars — including the possibility of a law enforcement vehicle. When I asked Mom about it a few times, she said that it was natural to be concerned about strangers in their area and that she and the other women spent the late afternoon and evening in the front room, visiting and "keeping an eye out." I often thought of what kind of pandemonium might occur if a strange car *had* driven up the long drive.

When one of my cousins was old enough and more experienced, he would be invited to join the poker-playing group. My oldest cousins, Sonny, Wilbert, Milford, Wayne, Eugene and Gilbert, never played, but Dale and Gene couldn't get to the table fast enough. They both had jobs and a little money to gamble. They learned to play the game by playing with the other cousins who stayed on these late Sunday afternoons. Gene had a special talent for the game and went on to become a professional poker player; by all indications, he did quite well. Incidentally, the gambling scenario was repeated on most holidays when the whole family got together — not just on Sundays.

The younger cousins would find an old deck of playing cards and, along with toothpicks or bottle caps for "money," sat on an open floor space and played "real" poker. The older kids among us enforced the rules, but if a question arose, we asked one of the older guys in the house who was not at the playing table. Under no circumstances did we disturb the men; this included those non-players huddled around the table.

The decks of cards we used were rarely complete, but we adjusted by either making one of the jokers the missing card, or just doing without. It didn't take long for even the youngest cousin to learn the nature of a poker deck and to also learn several different games of poker.

Later in my life as a high school teacher, several faculty members would get together late on Friday evenings and play poker most of the night. We all enjoyed this "penny ante" very much. It was extra special for me as I recalled my poker-playing days on the kitchen floor of the old farmhouse.

A straight flush!

🌿 34 🌿

Fireflies and Corncobs

It is early afternoon and, as I walk along the creek, I see several flashes of light under the heavy shade of the trees. Once the sun goes down, I bet we'll be able to catch a bunch of 'em.

Many of our favorite games were not played at school. Some were played at night, and others were considered too dangerous for the teacher to take chances on potential injuries. Except for throwing snowballs, baseballs and rubber balls, we could throw nothing else on school grounds. But throwing rocks on the way home and skipping them on ponds and creeks was great fun. Although quite heavy, hedge-balls, or Osage Oranges, were fun to heave, but we could get very little distance out of them or hit targets. At home, on the other hand, we could throw anything — from dried cow pies to walnuts to corncobs.

We made a kind of arrow or dart by using shucked corncobs that were made bare and soft. Feathers six inches in length or longer were inserted in the soft center of the stubby end of the cob. This provided stability so the cob could be thrown a rather great distance with considerable accuracy. Contests of all kinds were held, such as throwing the greatest distance — or throwing through rings made of wire or old iron wheels. The selection of the feathers was critical because longer feathers provided greater accuracy, but their air resistance decreased the distance. Since the grounds around the house showed the butchering sites of dozens of chickens, ducks and game fowl, just the right feather was often found. Many times these contests turned into throwing at each other until a parent put a stop to it. The constant fear of "putting an eye out" was always a reminder.

Summer nights brought millions of fireflies over the pastures, along the creek and into the yard. In the early evening, if we found a glass jar with a lid, we sneaked up as they flew by and captured them, either in our hands or directly into the jar. On several occasions, two or more of us went after the same firefly. If it were flying at a pretty high speed, and if we did not see our companions coming, we had quite a collision. Fence posts, wires, trees and other obstructions were also hazards on a dark night.

If we collected thirty or forty lightning bugs, we had enough light for an all-night adventure. We took them to a dark place, and with the random flashing of their tails, had a pretty steady light. Then, if we could convince our parents, we put them in our bedrooms, and the jar glowed all night. Most died before morning, but during the night one could actually see across the room. This worked especially well, since the only other nightlight in the house was a kerosene lamp or a candle.

We also learned to take a single firefly and rub its tail on our forehead — or on the back of our hand. The remaining material then glowed for several minutes. We extended this, on occasion, to wiping a band around one of our fingers and, just like magic, we had a beautiful glowing ring.

Dancing points of light.

35

Dogs and Cats

Pal jumps up and licks my face. His tail is wagging so hard that his back feet slip and he falls down. Even though he is just a puppy, he is learning how to help herd the cows. I hope he is careful not to come across any rattlesnakes.

Small animals provided a way of life on the farm. We always had at least two dogs and from four or five — to even fifteen or more cats. We seldom used a veterinarian even for the larger, profit-making animals; the small pets were born and died on a regular basis.

Our dogs were major friends and traveled with us to the fields and to the pastures to retrieve the milking cows. Since we lived on a gravel road, the dogs chased the occasional car as it traveled by. Inevitably, a car would hit them and they usually died. Some survived, with a broken leg or ribs, and even the loss of a leg. Another cause of death was from a rattlesnake bite either directly or from being "put down" with a gunshot. This was necessary to put them out of their misery if nothing else could be done. On rare occasions, if they got into the habit of finding and eating chicken eggs, they would be shot as well. This would cure them of "sucking eggs" as the expression went. Because of these hazards, dogs and cats seldom required euthanasia because of old age.

We never wasted a rifle bullet on any small animal except the dogs. When it was necessary, it was a very difficult time. We could all hear the shot from a distance. It was especially tough on Dad since he usually did the job. I could see the agony on his face as he returned from the field near the creek. I only remember this happening a few times during my life on the farm.

Cats, on the other hand, were great in number and were looked upon as helpers. They kept the mouse and rat population under some control. Sometimes, though, there were too many cats, so other measures had to be taken. Pop did not hesitate to send young kittens to the bottom of our nearby creek in a gunnysack weighted with rocks. He never told us of these events, and I never knew of anything showing up as evidence along or in the creek. We certainly knew that some of the cats were missing, however.

While we were milking, most of the cats would show up for a little treat, and the kids had great fun squirting milk from the cows' teats into the air and watching them jump for the stream, falling all over each other in the process. Some just closed their eyes and walked directly into the stream with their mouths open. We also provided them as much skim milk as they wanted each morning and evening after the milk separating was completed.

"Pal."

✿ 36 ✿

Wringing Their Necks

Mom says, "Try to catch that one!" She is pointing to a young rooster. I clutch my wire hook and sneak up slowly. As I get to within a few feet, I reach out with the wire and catch him by one foot and hang on. Mom runs over and grabs the chicken by the neck with one hand and traps the legs with the other.

Of all my memories of farm life, perhaps the most vivid and pleasant are of Mom walking through a flock of chickens throwing oats and other mixed grains over the ground for their feed. They followed her so politely and would cackle softly as a group. Mom responded by singing to them. While this seemed an amiable relationship, chickens on the farm either had to produce eggs or were eaten or sold. Only on very rare occasions did one self-select and become a pet.

Chicken-butchering time on the farm involved at least one parent and one kid. When a couple of buckets of boiling water were on the kitchen stove, the announcement was made that it was time to get the chicken. I ran outside to get the long, stiff wire that hung on the side of the porch. It was about four or five feet long, and had a hook bent at one end at just the right angle and size to snag the leg of a chicken and hold it. While this was going on, out in the yard the chickens freely pecked the ground for food. When Mom or Dad declared which bird would be our next feast, I carefully crept toward it and, after a few minutes, lunged with the wire and hobbled the fryer by one leg. I pulled back with all my strength and drew it near me as it struggled, cackled loudly and flapped its wings violently. Then Mom grabbed the chicken by the head and feet and placed it on a stump of wood. The neck was placed between two vertical nails driven into the stump about one or two inches apart. By pulling back on the feet, the chicken lengthened out for a quick chop of the ax! When released, it invariably fell off the log and, with blood spattering everywhere, ran in circles or sometimes across the yard. It was easy to see where the expression, "running around like a chicken with his head cut off," came from and, to this day, I sometimes still use it. After a short time, the stump was cleaned by rain and sunshine and ready for the next victim. We used this process with bigger fowl such as ducks, geese and guineas. However, if Dad were in charge of killing a chicken, he eliminated the block phase and simply swung the chicken by its head in circles at arm's length. When the head came off, the result was the same. The chicken would hit the ground running, and Dad had to dodge the spurts of blood. The saying, "wringing your neck," was also common in those days and expressed a threat when something was in dispute between two parties.

The next step was to lift the chicken off the ground by its feet and dip it into a bucket of boiling water carried out from the kitchen. The timing of the dips was critical since too much heat would affect the meat — and it would not be as tasty. The strong smell of hot, wet feathers was unpleasant and is impossible to forget. After a few dips, the larger feathers could be pulled off and thrown to the ground. They eventually blew around for a day or so and disappeared. Another dipping loosened the next layer of feathers. My sister and I would then finish pulling the smaller, finer feathers, or the down, if we were cleaning ducks. This was a very boring job disliked by everyone. Occasionally, another bucket of boiling water was added if the first one cooled too quickly. With that task completed, the chicken was gutted and the inside rinsed out. Most of the entrails were saved to eat. These included heart, liver and gizzard. The gizzard was carefully sliced open to shell out the sand and gravel accumulated to aid in the chicken's digestion. In later years, when teaching historical geology, I related this experience with my description of a similar organ in dinosaurs — except the gizzard stones or gastroliths of the dinosaurs were as large as three inches across. The chicken's feet were skinned, the nails cut-off, and included in the final product for baking. Further, the head was retrieved and carefully trimmed with any eatable parts, such as the brain, retained for cooking.

We then took the chicken inside, removed the wood-stove lid, and lighted a piece of paper for an instant flame. The chicken was rotated above the flame to singe away the rest of the feather stubs. Another disagreeable odor that has lingered in my memory through the decades is of singed feathers over an open flame. If a black coating were formed here or there on the carcass, Mom washed it with soap and warm water. Now the bird was sparkling clean and ready for the oven. This involved several other preparations.

Baking was done in a large open pan looking somewhat like a cookie sheet with a narrow rim. The carcass and parts were placed into the pan with a little water. With just an occasional check to baste the chicken, the primary problem was to maintain a proper temperature in the oven situated right next to the wood-burning chamber of the stove. Controlling the burning wood during the baking process required the oven door to be lowered occasionally to regulate the temperature. Although milk could initially supplement the baking chicken, it was generally added later to prepare chicken gravy for bread and potatoes with the meal.

When we expected a large number of friends and relatives, as many as six or eight chickens would be prepared for one large meal. Neatly centered on our large oak table, the vivid memory of several platters of golden fried chicken surrounding a platter of fried yellow chicken feet remains with me.

"Pop's" place today.

37

Hog Butchering Time

As I jump out of bed, I can smell the smoke coming from the fire my dad just started. I run to the window and look out at Mom and Dad and some of my uncles placing large barrels of water over the fire. We'll be butchering hogs today!

When the time came to butcher a hog, preparations started many days earlier. Barrels for boiling water — as well as the fire trough — had to be acquired either directly from their storage place in the barn or borrowed from a neighbor. Knives and axes were sharpened; arrangements for as much help as possible were made with relatives and neighbors. We selected the hog several months before the big day and gave it special care. The kids generally had the responsibility of spending a little extra time feeding enriched grain mixes to the animal.

The hogs were isolated in a smaller pen when butchering day approached. This made it easier to keep the animal close to the slaughter area. Pigs were generally killed with a single bullet in the front of the head through the center cavity, leaving the edible brains on either side undamaged. Uncle Carl did that job by a single-shot rifle and a .22 short rifle bullet.

Next Dad would slit its throat. After the animal bled for a

time, often into a large bucket, its back legs were tied together and, with a pulley system, the pig was hoisted to a high branch in a tree at the site. The whole animal was then lowered into a nearby barrel of boiling water to get the hair soft enough to scrape off. After a few dips — much like when cleaning chickens — the pig was lowered onto the ground — which was covered with gunnysacks or papers. At this point, with the animal steaming hot, the kids started to scrape off the hair. This was done with small empty fruit or soup cans. They crawled up on the hog and, by pushing hard on the open end of a can, and circling it around an area of the surface, the hair was rubbed off. This seemed to take forever; in actuality the dead pig was nearly bare after only an hour or so. Of course, adults always had to do touch-ups on the hard-to-get-at places. Then the pig was lifted up again. A large tub was placed below the animal and it was quickly gutted. The hog was then pulled up with ropes and pulleys to a high limb of the tree to cool. It stayed there overnight and remained seven or eight feet high so the dogs couldn't reach it.

The next day, we used saws and knives to quickly piece out the hog. We saved everything possible, including the entrails. We separated different parts into various pans and jars and stored them for processing. Even the head was severed from the body and the eyes removed. The "snout," consisting of the nose, jaws and teeth, was sawed off vertically across the front. Only the tongue was saved from this part. The dogs had a frenzied time when the adults threw the snout across the yard. It soon disappeared from view amid the excited barking of the dogs.

When the entrails and stomach were pulled from the catch tub, the cleaning process began. After considerable scrubbing with cold water, we cut the entrails into large segments several feet long.

This made them easier to clean because they were pulled inside out to expose the inner surface for continued scrubbing. The resulting sheath then served as a casing for various lunchmeat and sausage rings. Using a hand-powered crank, ground meat was pressed into a chamber a few inches in diameter and squeezed out of a lower tube fitted with the cleaned entrails. The length of the tube of this sausage varied as the ends were tied off with string. Sometimes the tube was long enough to form a nearly complete circle — a foot or so in diameter — by tying both ends together. This made it easier to hang on nails or pegs. Placed in a smoke house for several weeks, this process produced a wonderful smoked sausage.

The rendering of lard from various largely fat sections of the hog took considerable time and effort, mostly in the kitchen on the wood-burning stove. The crisp pieces rendered from skin fat are called cracklings; they were very tasty and, to this day, are a special treat.

The head was "worked" by using a meat grinder with a very fine setting. With the exception of the brains, preserved separately as a delicacy, all possible edible parts of the head were used in this process including the jowls and the skin. The resulting "head" sausage was sometimes mixed with the blood saved from the initial bleeding. Aunt Nettie specialized in cleaning and preparing the hog's stomach to act as the casing for this blood sausage. After being packed tightly into the stomach, with the openings sewn together with string, the bundle cooked slowly in a large kettle of water for a few hours until done. Once cooled and stored for future use, these sausages, sometimes called lunchmeat, would be consumed by slicing the required amount from the tube or stomach pack and either reheating or eating cold. The blood sausage sliced bright red!

Another kind of sausage was prepared by adding liver to the "head sausage." Liver sausage tasted best of all sausages. The tongue and other special parts like the heart, liver and brains were also treated separately and packaged for future use.

As the fall progressed, Mom finally had time to prepare large quantities of pork meatballs, pickled pigs' feet, cracklings and pork chops. The meatballs, cracklings and chops were packed in large crocks, layered with lard for preservation until use. The feet were kept in glass jars. These pork products, along with potatoes from our garden, were then stored in the cellar below the kitchen, and provided regular meals throughout the winter months.

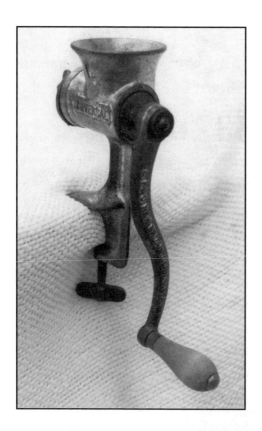

Meat grinder.

Ten-gallon crock.

38

Milkweed and Rattlesnakes

It's fun starting the day with a hoe that Dad has just sharpened. The blade is so shiny. As I cut the thick stalk, white stuff, which looks like milk, oozes out. I tasted it once. It was awful!

During the long summer days, a continuing responsibility of the entire family was to hoe milkweed, morning glories, bind weed, sunflowers, volunteer corn and cockleburs from the cornfields. During cool morning hours we packed lunches, filled water buckets with fresh water from the well, and loaded everything into a rack wagon pulled by an old Allis-Chalmers tractor. Dad always spent whatever spare moments he could find in sharpening tools in the shop so the hoe blades glistened in the sun as we began our day's work. The local farmers took great pride in the condition of the fields. My dad was very critical of any field that was not clean of weeds. He considered it a symptom of laziness and expected our fields to be weed-free — as well as those of our neighbors.

After arriving at the field, we would unload our tools, and each of us was assigned a corn row to hoe at one edge of the field. Depending on the growth of their own crops, another nearby family might "trade labor" and join us for a day or two. We sometimes had eight to ten men, women and children hoeing at one time. There were no portable bathrooms in those days, so we simply looked for a private place in the cornfield or nearby timber.

For the kids, these fields looked like great expanses of land, the endless corn rows stretching to infinity. Dad always picked a few rows between the kids somewhere so that he had a little control of our work and, looking back, our safety. Once we got just a little ways into the field, sights and sounds of the countryside disappeared and, with the corn above our heads by several feet, we found ourselves totally alone. Within an hour or so, the temperature rose and the sweat started to flow. No wind or breeze reached us within the high stocks of corn, and the smell of the damp ground and the growing corn was unlike that encountered anywhere else.

We often saw snakes in front of us in the cornrow. If we recognized it as a rattlesnake, we let out a scream and Dad came running. He often tracked it down and chopped the head off with the hoe. He then snipped off the rattles, put them in his pocket and draped the snake's body over the nearest wire fence. This very strong custom was believed to help produce a good rain within the next few days. I do not recall that this worked — but he always did it. He then returned to us and buried the head deeply in the part of the corn row that we had already groomed. We tried to remember exactly where they were buried from one time to the next, but that wasn't very successful. The old-timers said that the snake's venom lasted for several days in the fangs, and we "dare not step on the head" as we might still get bitten by the dead snake.

Although we could not see the other end of the row, we continued to hoe weed after weed with the thought of a dipper of water that waited for us at the far end. Walking and hoeing at a regular pace along one of the rows might take as long as twenty-five to thirty minutes. Dad showed up to inspect our progress, and almost always found a weed or two that we missed. Then he disappeared again to hoe along his own rows.

Cockleburs were by far the most plentiful weed, but sunflowers were the most stubborn. It took a mighty chop to cut through their thick stems. If we had a weed preference, it would be the milkweed. With just a gentle slice, the soft-stemmed weed seeped a white, milky substance at both surfaces. If we could retrieve the top portion of the weed for cattle and pigs, it made a welcome treat for them at the end of the day.

Arriving at the end of the row produced the expected drink of water and, for some of the older kids and most of the adults, it was time for a smoke from a hand-rolled cigarette. Almost everyone but the younger kids smoked in those days. This pause also gave me a little time to observe other people who were working in the fields. The men all wore overalls and long-sleeved shirts. It was quite a spectacle to see these guys as they relaxed without their hats, with their white foreheads shining in the light, and their graceful way of striking matches on the brass buttons of their overalls. They also showed great skill and technique as they blew their noses; by placing a forefinger against one nostril, they turned their head, leaned over and blew out the other nostril!

One of the greatest scares we encountered during those farm days was my passing out near the end of a corn row on an extremely hot, sticky day. I barely remember Dad finding me on the ground; I was completely weak and made no movement at all. He took me to the only shade — under the hay wagon. Mom was also out in the fields, and used water on a rag to cool my head. After a period of an hour or two, I felt much better and we stopped work and headed for home. This was the last time that my sister and I had to spend full, long days hoeing in the fields. From then on, we rode out with Mom later in the morning to deliver lunch, and the three of us helped the crew for just a few hours at midday.

If Dad arrived home in the evening with some rattlesnake rattles in his pocket, he would attach them to the underside of his banjo. This added a unique and interesting hum when the banjo was played. I have that banjo today with some rattles still attached!

Rattlesnake nearby!

39

Christmas on Our Very Own Farm

Now when Jesus was born in Bethlehem of Judaea in the days of Herod the king … Mom, what comes next? "Behold, there came wise men from the east to Jerusalem," Mom says. This is really tough. I am never going to learn my piece.

During the late fall of our first year at Pop's place, an eighty-acre farm located just a mile to the northwest came up for sale. It was owned by relatives on my grandmother's side of the family. They were moving to a slightly larger place nearby and gave us the opportunity to have a farm of our own. Our expectations that my dad would be drafted had diminished that fall. With the impending defeat of Germany and the invasion force ready to strike Japan, the draft board's quota had no intention of calling up a 37-year-old married farmer. Dad borrowed the few thousand-dollar purchase price and we moved in within a day or two. The house had been built just a few years earlier, but it had no more conveniences than the home place. An outdoor toilet, no running water, no electricity and three small bedrooms, all on one floor, would describe this little house. The road past the house was not heavily traveled and had very little gravel covering it. Getting stuck in the mud was a regular occurrence whether driving our car or tractor or just walking. The distance from Stony Ridge School was just about the same as before, but it was now a straight shot with no turns or jogs. Along the lane leading to the new home were apple and cherry trees. Their blossoms that spring became a lasting memory.

Soon after we moved to the new farm, we had a large Thanksgiving dinner at Pop's place. The dinner of fried chicken, corn, mashed potatoes and gravy was attended by most of our relatives in the area and Mom's cooking was a hit.

At about this same time, Uncle Carl and Aunt Clara decided to move back in with Pop. Their son, Edgar, enrolled at Stony Ridge and brought the attendance up to five. This was beginning to be just like a real school with enough kids to enjoy recesses and to have group activities.

The anticipation of Christmas excited us greatly when we cut down one of the few six-foot cedars near our new house for our Christmas tree. Over the course of several late afternoons and early evenings, Mom popped corn over the wood stove and, using a sewing needle, we strung the kernels on string. We wrapped the tree with ten or twelve-foot strands. We also made paper chains out of strips of newspaper. As we had done at school, a mixture of flour and water provided the paste and, with a few crayons, these chains provided a nice color decoration.

In church at Christmas time, each of the Sunday school kids had to learn a "piece." As younger kids, my sister and I only had to memorize a small sentence from the Biblical story of Christ's birth. The older kids had several verses from the Bible and would, each year, receive a different verse from the previous year. This provided us with a little more understanding and appreciation of the Bible. After we received our sentence on a little piece of paper, we had to practice for a few weeks at home. Then, at only one rehearsal, we tried to put it all together. We went through the entire program two times at this one setting. What a long and tedious Sunday afternoon that was! My sister, who is two years younger, memorized her piece in just a day or so. I had a much more difficult time. Most of the kids were not ready at the rehearsal, but it all seemed to come together when we presented the actual program.

At least half of our Sunday school time each week — leading up to the performance — involved memorizing the music that we all sang together. The Christmas songs, *Away in a Manger, Silent Night* and *O, Little Town of Bethlehem* were featured each year. These wonderful tunes have been sung or hummed every Christmas season since those exciting school-time days.

Since the younger kids spoke their parts first, my sister opened the program with her appearance on the stage and had no difficulty. In anticipation of my first experience in front of a crowd, I do not recall being particularly nervous. When my turn came to walk to the center of the stage, however, I froze. Looking over the large crowd of faces, I finally saw my mom and dad about halfway down the center isle. I broke into tears and ran to them and spent the rest of the evening in Mom's arms. Unlike today, the kids on the farm had little contact with anyone other than the few kids in school and their immediate families. Shyness and uncertainty when around crowds of strangers was common. But no one seemed at all disturbed with my tearful reaction. When the program was over, we all filed out. The men at the exit door handed us sacks of candy with peanuts; a little hard, wavy red, green and white candy; and an orange at the top. I was handed one along with everyone else. In my mind, that positive reception indicated that I was still accepted even after such a disaster. Later during my lifetime, I worked very hard to become comfortable in large crowds and when speaking in front of groups.

When we got home from the program, my parents suggested that we stay in the car for a few minutes until they got the lanterns lighted in the house. From the car, we could see the light go on in the front room windows and, after a few more minutes, Mom came out to get us. They had a great surprise! Santa Claus had come by while we were in church. As we rushed in, we noticed several brightly wrapped presents under the tree. Mom and Dad each had one and my sister and I each had two or three.

My sister made an unfortunate discovery early in the Christmas season of that year. She explored the closets and found a doll's cradle in Mom's closet. With great excitement, she brought it out to show Mom what she had found! It was one of her Christmas presents. Mom told her that it was for Christmas and that it had to be put back where she found it. No explanation was given at the time, except that Santa didn't always bring all the presents. Sometimes Mom and Dad would get something special for us as well. Although giving Santa Claus full credit for the gifts, it was probably the last Christmas that I truly believed in him.

A long, heavy package was handed to me, and inside was an official major league baseball bat — the most memorable present of my life. I was totally surprised, and to this day I can smell the special hickory varnish finish of that factory-made bat. I took it to bed with me that night, but was too excited to sleep. With bad weather over the next few days, I grew impatient of waiting to try it out. Finally, my dad and I had a great time together when I could hit an old taped-up ball that we had around the house.

Since it was a regulation bat, it required all my strength to swing it. I eventually grew into it and had some significant hits when I started to play town baseball several years later.

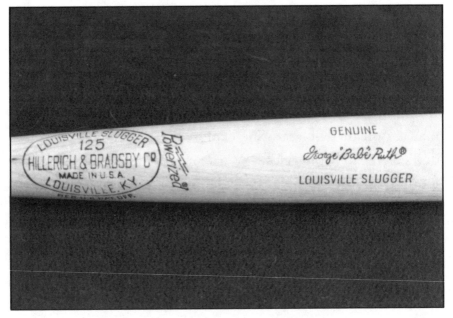

The most memorable gift of all.

40

The Stony Ridge Mountain Boys

As usual, we are about the first ones here. We drive off the road into Al Rathke's pasture where the baseball diamond is. Dad says he likes to park near the first base line where most of the outs are made. We can also see the batters' faces better.

From the time that Dad and I first started to play catch with a baseball, he shared many stories of playing for the Stony Ridge Mountain Boys baseball team. Primarily a pitcher, he also played third base, and carefully instructed me in these two positions.

I never saw Dad play, but we did watch a number of baseball games on the same field where he had played and, together, we watched some of my uncles and cousins play for the same team. The various teams in the county and surrounding area were called "town teams." Dad's team was formed by friends and neighbors from local farms. Actual towns sometimes represented themselves by name. But since many of the games were played either on the grounds of the country schools, or in Dad's case, on a diamond built on one of the player's farms, the teams often took their names after their nearby one-room school. With the school resting on the crest of the highest hill in the area, our team name became "The Stony Ridge Mountain Boys."

Games were played on Sunday afternoons, and many people came from the two rival communities. Very few players wore baseball gloves, and those who had them played on the infield only. To pay for baseballs, catcher's masks and chest protectors, a hat was passed among the spectators for donations. The support for the respective baseball teams was taken very seriously and everyone donated to the cause. I can remember my surprise when I spotted several dollar bills in the hat as it went by.

Only an occasional spectator watched the game from a chair. Instead, the fans drove their cars, and sometimes horse-drawn wagons, behind the tiny backstop — or parked around the outfield. When a team scored a run, the fans sounded their horns to create some real excitement on that bare, hot, treeless plain.

Dad told us about the last time he played for the team during the summer after I was born. He wore a Panama straw hat and batted against the most feared pitcher in the entire region. His name was Bill Ohm and was a distant cousin of my dad's. The Stony Ridge Mountain Boys was primarily a Schrader team, and my dad had just married into the family. The very first pitch was a high, hard fastball and, with hat flying, Dad ducked away, landing in a heap beside home plate. He got up, thinking it was a near miss, and retrieved his hat. To everyone's surprise, one edge of the hat's bill was completely missing. The ball had grazed the headband and sheared off the bill "as if it were cut by a knife." Since the ballplayer's clothing is officially considered a part of the player, the umpire ruled that Dad was hit by the ball and awarded him first base. No one was ever able to get Bill Ohm to admit that he had intentionally thrown at Dad's head; but it sure ended Dad's baseball career.

Watching baseball games with my dad during these very early

school days gave me the basis for a lifelong love of the game. In addition to playing baseball in high school and college, I started collecting baseball cards shortly after they first appeared on the newsstands and in grocery stores in 1948. I can remember opening my very first pack of cards and getting a Yogi Berra rookie card. Even though I have been tempted to sell that card over the years, I still have it. I collected baseball cards on a regular basis through my senior year in high school, and have actually owned some cards that have become quite valuable. Rookie cards of Hank Aaron and Roberto Clemente are still in my collection, although I have somehow misplaced, traded or ruined rookie cards of Mickey Mantle, Willie Mays and many others. We often clothespinned cards onto our bicycle spokes to simulate motorcycle engine sounds — and we lost a great number of cards and dollars in the process. Nevertheless, baseball has been a big part of my life, and I still watch it today with images of those hot summer days in the Flint Hills.

Stony Ridge Mountain Boys.

Front row, left to right: Leo Rathke Sr., pitcher and first baseman; Wilbert Hinrich, outfielder; Louis Rathke, catcher; Delbert Moran, short stop; Walter Rathke, pitcher and infielder.

Back row: Wayne Schroeder, third baseman; Dale Schroeder, infield utility player; Lawrence Gramke, first baseman; Gay Hinrich, catcher; Robert Rathke, pitcher and outfielder; William Rathke, outfielder; Chet Mackey, utility outfielder.

❧ 41 ❧

Noodling and the Swimming Hole

As I awaken, I'm sweating and sticking to the sheets. This is going to be a really hot day. I remember now — Dad said he will be noo-dling in the creek this afternoon. Maybe he will let me swim in a couple of water holes downstream from him.

Shaw Creek flowed within several hundred yards of our farm-house and provided three favorable swimming holes. Underground springs supplied an almost undetectable current. During the sum-mer and on weekends, with school in session, we frequently hur-ried down for a quick swim or splash in the warm, dark water. Seldom escorted by adults, we stripped to our underwear and dove or waded into the water.

Although the water, most of the time, compared to a warm bath, occasionally a very cold stream hit us from below. We swam or walked quickly away from that spring vent to get back into the warmth. We enjoyed swinging from the creek bank over the wa-ter on a rope which Dad had tied to a tree limb. We had contests to see who could swing the highest and jump the farthest into the water.

We often encountered underwater objects such as limbs, leaf clumps, apples and other fruit that had fallen from nearby trees.

On other occasions, the objects would move — on their own — and we knew that these most likely were some of the many fish also swimming in the hole.

On one hot summer day, I came up for air and opened my eyes to stare directly into the eyes of a water snake no more than ten feet away. With poisonous water moccasins and cottonmouths abundant in the area, I yelled and swam quickly in the opposite direction. Looking back to what had been only the snake's head above water, I saw the whole snake swimming away from me on top of the water. It produced a startling wake in the water shaped like a sine-wave. I remember exchanging stories with some of my cousins about being hit in the chest or stomach with something long and squirmy, which may well have been a snake!

We never carried towels, but let the warm winds dry us when we finished our swim. We also checked each other for leeches that might have attached during our swim. When we found one, we slowly pulled it off so that part of its head would not remain fastened to our skin. This was similar to removing a tick, although for ticks we generally waited until the end of the day. Our parents helped us by holding a hot glowing stick or a match close to the tick to make it release its hold. If this did not work, then we pulled it off slowly as we did with leeches.

We often walked to the creek bank to search for snakes swimming in the water. We gathered several pockets full of rocks to throw at them. They seemed to know when a rock was aimed at them, because they ducked under the water and, after the rock hit, immediately rose back to the surface. I do not remember any of us killing a single snake — or even scoring a direct hit.

In the spring, in contrast to the kids swimming in the creek for the fun of it, the men swam in the creek for another purpose.

My dad, or one of my uncles or older cousins, entered the water wearing a long-sleeved shirt, pants and socks and swam down to the cold water at the bottom of the deeper pools. The divers did not use oxygen tanks or fins of any kind. Although each dive lasted only a few minutes, it seemed much longer for the observers on shore. Along the edges of these underwater caverns were shelves of limestone, which had deep cavities within them. These, along with submerged hollow logs, were sometimes hiding places for large fish such as channel cats or blue cats.

The "noodler" moved along the edge, searching the crevices with his arms and hands in the hope of finding a large catfish. When they found one, they quickly placed a fist into the mouth or grabbed it through the gills and pulled it out of the hole. Unless this were done quickly, the fish could sometimes extend its fins against the fissure — making it impossible to pull the fish out. If the fish did not let go, the noodler could easily drown. The fish could also charge out of the hole, slamming the swimmer in the chest. When the successful catch came up to the surface, the men remaining on the bank waded in to help land the fish. This was great adventure, and a successful "noodle" would be talked about for weeks.

Plentiful stories about various noodling incidents involved fish so big that the swimmer had to resort to great measures to survive — and be able to swim back to safety. The noodler might also find a very large turtle or a snake in the underwater caverns. It was said that if a searching hand encountered the wrong end of a snapping turtle, it might bite down on a finger or two. The noodler then had to pull the turtle to the surface or suffer the consequences. Once on the creek bank, the fingers could only be released by cutting away the jaws of the turtle!

I remember seeing some of my relatives with skin stripped from their arms and hands after one of these adventures. In church or at baseball games, I observed a number of older men with scarred hands — some had lost a finger or two or were without a hand or an arm. I was told that they were injured either by a hay-bailer or in a noodling accident. That vision made a lasting impression!

The swimming hole.

❧ 42 ❧

Bullheads and Sunfish

I am sitting on an old tree trunk by the side of the creek. Mom, Dad and cousin Herman intently fish around the bend. I am totally alone. My cork floats motionless in the water just a few feet from me. It is very hot and still in the shade of the giant oak trees overhead, and the smell of dead fish is awful. Water bugs scurry across the quiet water — I wonder what is down below!

If we encountered an unusual number of underwater creatures while swimming in the nearby creek, we ran up the hill to the barn for our fishing poles. We made poles from the green limbs of nearby trees. These poles were about six feet long, approximately straight, with slight bends here and there along the length. We tied a string about seven feet long to the narrow end, and Dad gave us an old, but real, factory-made hook to tie to the other end. We generally used a stick to act as a floater, but later some of us used a real cork for that purpose.

Finding a place to sit on the edge of the creek bank presented the most challenging part of the whole experience. With heavy shade from the surrounding trees, the sloping banks were seldom completely dry. They were muddy, slick and dangerous. We slid down to the water's edge and grabbed on to twigs or grass to slow

157

or stop the fall. Surprisingly, we did not slide into the water very often.

We dug worms for bait near the windmill by the creek. Turning a couple of small boards over in the dirt exposed night crawlers and other smaller worms. We seldom used a full worm — choosing instead to pull them in half before sticking them on the hook. We also caught grasshoppers if it did not take too much time and effort. Sometimes they seemed quite sluggish, and we sneaked up and grabbed them — while other times they were impossible to catch. While we held them in our fingers, they would spit out a brown substance we called tobacco. We smeared it back over their bodies and then spit on them before placing a hook through their torso.

From the creek bank, we tossed the baited hook out as far as we could into the dark water and waited patiently for a "bite." The bobber stick or cork would indicate some nibbles, and we knew that we might have some excitement. Crayfish (or "crawdads") and turtles frequently nibbled on the bait giving us false hope. When the bobber sank completely under water, we jerked up the far end of the pole as quickly as we could and swung the catch to the bank. If it were a turtle, we generally had difficulty removing the hook and would have to cut the line before throwing it back into the creek. On more than one occasion, we caught a turtle that had an old hook in its mouth.

Crawdads were easy to free from the hook. We simply grabbed one from behind the claws so it could not pinch us. When Dad or other adults fished, they cut up the crawdad and used the pieces for bait. I do not recall any real success with this kind of bait, but it offered an exciting alternative.

My sister swam very little, but she really liked to join us for a fishing trip. The boys always tried to catch a big bullhead, but my sister was content with sunfish and, looking back, had great fun catching more than we caught. She probably could catch four or five sunfish to our single bullhead. When she had a slow fishing day, we liked to kid her about why her fish line's bobber was dry! Since she had no bites that day, this teasing bothered her at first, but she soon got used to it. To this day, I like to remind her of her dry bobber.

Cleaning bullheads proved a rather tough job for kids. Dad showed us how to hold the bullhead behind the front "stingers," hit the head of the fish with a hammer a few times to kill it — or at least knock it out — and then cut the skin around the lower part of the head. Gutting was generally done near the creek where the entrails could be spilled on the ground; wild animals ate them after we left. Then we used pliers to strip the skin from the neck to the tail. Three or four strips were all that we needed to get the meat ready for the frying pan. Then we cut off the head and buried it. The stingers could really hurt if stepped on with bare feet.

We cleaned sunfish more quickly with gutting done first; then we scraped off the scales with a sharp knife before beheading. On occasion, we skinned the sunfish as we did the catfish, but the meat held on more tightly to the skin, and the resulting filet was not nearly as appetizing.

The final step on a successful fishing day included wandering around the kitchen — taking in the wonderful aromas, as Mom prepared these gastronomical delights. Tiny bones had to be carefully removed before eating. Then we all looked forward to a leisurely meal. Leftovers were not plentiful but, when they were, everyone enjoyed cold fish from the icebox.

A nice bullhead.

🌰 43 🌰

Ghost Stories

About eight of us gather in the pantry this evening. We sit down on the floor in a circle and someone shuts the door. It is very dark and quiet. Larry starts out with a story about a chain dragging across the ceiling in the haymow. It isn't very scary — maybe we can get Darrell to come in to tell us one of his really scary stories. When the door is opened, I see that Edgar has his arm around Carolyn. What is going on?

At the end of the first leg of our walk to school from Pop's place, we turned to the right for another half mile. At this junction, nearly hidden in the trees, stood an old deserted stone house. Others told us not to venture off the road or go near the house because it appeared very old and unsafe.

But we knew another reason, as we had heard many stories about the strange people who had once lived there. Supposedly they buried one of their children directly under the stone slab used as a step to the door on the west side. The child, a six-year-old girl, was buried in a long white dress. Not only did all my cousins know — and believe — the story but, when visiting with kids from other one-room schools, the story was told quite consistently. Before and after Sunday school, we told the tale over and over, with many details filled in by knowing older kids.

161

General consensus recounted that the little girl died of natural causes during the flu epidemic of 1917. The parents, too poor and heartbroken to have a "proper" burial, decided to keep her close to them. From then on, several people reported that while driving or walking past the house on moonlit nights, they saw flashes of white weaving through the treetops. Many also claimed to hear a high, wailing cry at the same time as the sightings. Some of the older kids spoke of planning to visit the old place — to find and lift up the stone step. But this never happened to my knowledge — it would have been too frightening to actually carry out such a plan.

During weekend evenings, the younger cousins sometimes gathered in the pantry near the kitchen at Pop's place. They tightly shut the door and created a very dark place to exchange ghost stories. We could sometimes talk our older cousin, Darrell, into being our storyteller and sharing some of his favorite stories. Although only thirteen years old, he had a deep, convincing voice.

He most often told the story of a local farmer who had his arm torn off by a hay bailer. The graphic details of the accident during the first part of the story helped to set us up for what followed. The man became so distraught over losing his arm that he sold his farm, livestock and machinery for enough money to buy a replacement arm. He finally chose an arm of pure gold and proudly wore it in public where people could see it.

Eventually, hoodlums found him alone one night, killed him and stole his golden arm. Within a few days, the robbers were all found dead with their skulls crushed — yet no one found a golden arm. The arm apparently was able to walk on its fingers during the night hoping to find its owner, and made regular trips into homes all over the area resting under children's beds. Children were not to look under their beds, as the golden arm did not want to be seen. "The Man with the Golden Arm" was a favorite folktale and, to this day, my cousins still relate variations of the story to their own children.

Our haunted house.

44

Trapping and Skinning

My feet are really cold. I must have stepped through some ice. So far, I've checked five traps and only have one little possum. I'm glad he was already dead. I only have a stick with which to kill 'em!

When deep winter really set in, animals developed thick coats of fur, and it would be time to try some trapping. Trapping was a very lucrative business during my parents' day — especially for school-age children. But when I first tried to trap, the animals were much more scarce, and it took a great deal of effort to catch them.

I would set three or four traps in the evening after I finished my chores. This was a cold and wet job as the traps were generally set along the creek. If the water were not frozen, the wet mud caused me to slip on the creek bank into the water.

I tried to trap raccoons, beavers or muskrats. They earned about fifty cents per hide and provided a rewarding celebration for the entire family. When I brought one home, Dad helped me skin it or skinned it himself, and generally nailed the pelt to a board on the side of the barn. They had to be well-dried or packed in salt before taking them into town to sell at a filling station in Olpe. Occasionally, I caught coyotes, skunks, or a small, spotted skunk called a civet. The skins earned varying prices according to the demands of the time — and they occasionally brought a dollar for a single skin.

The selling of the coyote was slightly different, however, because we only had to produce the two ears to receive a fifty-cent bounty. The state government encouraged this method to get rid of a livestock threat. Sometimes we used cyanide-laced bait to poison coyotes if they ventured too close to the chicken house or threatened small calves or pigs. After removing the ears, we just left the carcass in the field for the vultures since the fur had no value.

I made the rounds after chores in the morning and checked every trap before the walk to school. I didn't carry a gun, but if I found a live animal in the trap, I would kill it with a blow to the head from a large stick that I carried. I frequently discovered a most disturbing scene when I came across a leg of an animal in the trap; it had been chewed off, allowing the animal to escape on three legs! This happened on several occasions, and I have never forgotten those incidents.

My rationale for this activity was simply that we needed the money. My older cousins spent many nights hunting coons with their dogs and spoke of the great adventure when treeing a coon high above the ground. I never participated in that kind of hunt, but later in my life I hunted a great deal, again for the food it supplied. I never really liked it and never developed the sense of detachment that many of my friends appeared to have when hunting or trapping.

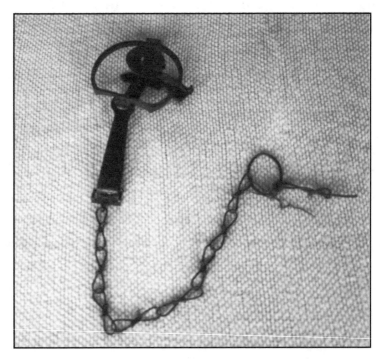

A steel trap.

❧ 45 ❧

Hedgerows and Rabbits

"Look real close, right over there," Dad says. He stretches his right arm in front of me and directs my gaze out the window to the base of a hedge tree. There in the snow are two rabbit ears, motionless and sticking straight up. I tremble a little as Dad sticks the single-shot .410 out the window and flips off the safety.

Dad waited until the second snow of the winter before he felt that rabbits were free of rabbit fever and were safe to hunt. In the early season, the rabbits were scattered all across our farmland, and Dad and I walked the grassy fields to scare them up. Although our dogs walked alongside us, they had no training to help in the hunt and took very little interest — other than sniffing the kill.

I carried my single-shot BB gun with a few lead BBs as ammunition. Dad carried a single-shot .410 gauge shotgun. My first memory of the little shotgun was when we lived in Winfield. It was so very beautiful and Dad allowed me to hold it and pretend to shoot — although never with my finger on the trigger. He cleaned that gun and a .22 caliber rifle with great love and attention. I think it provided a kind of therapy for him. When taking the bolt out of both guns, we looked up the barrel at a light bulb hanging in the kitchen to see the spiraled rifling grooves. These were exciting times, and I had visions of someday actually hunting with these same guns.

Dad was very cautious and took his job of teaching me hunting very seriously. Gun safety was the primary goal from the moment we started the hunt. Although I played with my BB gun almost every day and shot all kinds of targets and birds, I discovered that a real hunt required serious concentration. Dad constantly reminded me that the barrel of the gun was to be pointed skyward or to the ground — and absolutely not to point it at another person! When crawling over fences and opening and shutting gates, he reminded me over and over what to do with the weapon. I had to discuss with Dad the various causes of an accident — either dropping the rifle or letting it fall from its leaning position against a fencepost or wire. If there were any chance that the gun would come in contact with the ground, I had to inspect it carefully to see that no dirt had entered the barrel. Although my BB gun had no safety mechanism, Dad showed me how to work it on the shotgun.

The winter finally got so severe that the rabbits hid in the hedgerows for protection. When walking through the fields along the hedgerows, before heavy snows, we found them hiding nearby in the dark hedge. After shooting them, we placed their heads under one of our shoes, grabbed their hind feet and pulled hard. Their heads came off, and the rabbit bled for a several seconds. If it were cold enough, we piled them together in one place until returning to take them home to clean.

After a snowstorm, we searched the hedgerows from our car. We dressed very warmly, almost as if we were walking the hedgerows. The shooter, on the passenger side, aimed the shotgun out the window. With the cold wind blowing into the open window, we drove slowly along the road while watching the hedgerow for rabbits hiding in the deep snow. They showed up as a dark silhouette and made easy targets. We believed it unlawful to shoot from the car, but Dad was afraid that opening the door and getting out would scare the rabbits. We harvested hundreds of them over the years — directly from the car seat.

Cleaning ten to twenty rabbits was quite a chore. Regardless of the time of year that we hunted them, Dad worried that they might have tularemia, or rabbit fever. We did not have rubber gloves or other protective clothing — and certainly no antibiotics were available in the early 1940s. He had a boyhood friend die of what was believed to be rabbit fever. Dad repeatedly reminded us that the disease could be transmitted to us if we were scratched by a broken bone. He said to tell him immediately if we saw one and he would dispose of it. Dad also told us to watch for any redness around scratches that we might get while cleaning rabbits or any other game.

Although Mom occasionally came along with us on the hunt, she never carried a gun. On one special day, however, she spotted a rabbit in the backyard of our farmhouse, and quickly retrieved the .410 and a couple of shells. She fired one time and, when retrieving the kill, found two dead rabbits instead of one. That evening she baked them with cream and prepared white gravy over a slice of bread. What a great meal we had! And what a story we told over and over throughout the years.

As I got older, the .410 shotgun eventually became mine, and I shot my first rabbit, squirrel, duck, quail, dove, prairie chicken and pheasant with it. While in junior high school, I completely refinished the stock and, to this day, it is still a prized possession.

Looking for rabbits in the hedgerow.

46

Duck Ponds

I'm in the back seat. Dad left some time ago and I'm getting hungry. I know Mom packed ham sandwiches and hot cocoa. We are on a high hill, just out of sight of the duck pond below. I see Mom running back from her viewing point. As she quietly enters the car, she whispers, "I saw Dad and he is close to the ducks and they don't see him yet. I bet he gets a bunch!"

Although we hunted rabbits all through the winter, ducks had a limited season. In the early fall, we heard the honking sounds of ducks and geese flying south. Winter would soon arrive. There were days when thousands of ducks would fill the sky, flying in long, meandering, "V"-shaped formations. At night, with no radio or other noises, we ran outside when we heard their honking to see them cross the moon or break starlight. This grand sight was incredibly fascinating to a youngster like me. How did the ducks know where they were going, and what special innate talent or skill did the leading duck possess, at the tip of the "V"?

At one time or another during the season, ducks and geese landed on most of the many ponds in the area. We had two ponds very close to our house and could see them after just a short walk. In the early morning sunrise, Dad and Mom prepared for the hunt. Dressed warmly and wearing rubber boots, Dad quietly sneaked out the door and walked or sometimes crawled to the base of the dam of one of the ponds. If he heard noise, he loaded the 16-guage shotgun with three or more shells and crept up the slope to the top of the dam. He fired the first shots before the birds left the water. Then it was a matter of getting off as many shots as he could before the ducks flew out of reach.

Dad had good days and bad days while shooting ducks and geese. Sometimes he brought home as many as three or four birds. At other times, he missed all his shots and would declare that he had been "skunked." And there were times when he peeked over the dam only to find not even a single duck on the pond. How they flew away without anyone seeing them was always a mystery.

If the two local ponds were empty of ducks, we frequently drove out to other ponds in our car. We packed sandwiches, hot coffee and chocolate along with blankets and pillows. After driving a few rocky miles through the flint hills, we finally arrived on a hilltop. From there we looked down over a number of ponds on our property and of our neighbor's. Mom had an incredible ability to see ducks on the ponds before the rest of us could. Dad and my sister also saw them as she pointed them out, but I never could. This should have hinted to all of us that my eyesight was poor, but we did not see an eye doctor until I finally got eyeglasses in junior high school.

Once the ducks or geese were spotted, Dad took out the shotgun and slowly, quietly moved from the car. He had to either get upwind or behind the dam without the ducks hearing or seeing him. Sometimes, we watched him crawl perhaps a hundred yards or more to get to the right spot. It was a very slow process, but Mom, my sister and I enjoyed the adventure.

If several ducks were brought back to the car, the excitement and satisfaction was very high. At times, a dead duck or two still floated on the pond. And Mom and Dad walked down and waited for the wind to blow them ashore — again a very exciting time for my sister and me. If no ducks were killed, Dad would spend several minutes discussing the reasons — and then we drove to the next pond.

These early hunting experiences started a string of many years where my personal schedule was centered around various hunting seasons. While living in Wyoming, I hunted and killed antelope, deer, elk and moose. Many of these hunts were with my father during his later years. I also hunted wild turkey and bear. But, for some reason, almost over-night, I suddenly found no interest whatsoever in hunting. This happened in my fortieth year, and I have not hunted since. I often wonder what my father would say, as he so loved the sport and gave me such a wonderful start.

My trusty .410.

47

Dust Storms

I can feel the dust in my eyes as well as its taste in my mouth. Mom walks over with a wet washrag to place over my mouth. She says, "Breathe through this for awhile. It should help and maybe the storm will be over before long." As I look across the front room, I see dust floating in the deep reddish-brown light and falling on the furniture and floor. The miserable afternoon stretches on and on, and all we can do is sit and wait.

A perfect summer day; not a cloud in the sky! Then, suddenly, we spotted a dark brown cloud low in the west. It extended clear across the horizon from north to south. Mom and Dad quickly determined that we were in for one of our occasional unruly visitors — so we immediately prepared for some hardship and lots of work.

Our teacher told us to stay in the building if a dust storm would soon arrive. If we were on the way home and caught in the dust, she told us to find a fence line and follow it. When we rode in a car, we could not see the roadway very well, and the car plowed through dust drifts reminding us of snow in the winter.

We could not determine how severe a dust storm would be, nor how long it would last. Some might linger for several days, while others would pass by in a few hours. We usually gathered towels and rags and soaked them with water. We placed them on each windowsill and worked small pieces along the side and top of the windows inside the house. We protected the back door in a similar way, but kept the front door free until just before the storm hit. This generally came about thirty minutes after we spotted the cloud. Dad, in the meantime, hurried to the livestock in the barnyard to get the animals safely inside. On his way back, he carried a few buckets of water from the well. He also covered the well so that it would be protected in the event that the storm lasted for several days.

The billowing clouds of dust swirled threateningly by high winds, and while it greatly excited the kids, it depressed the adults. When the storm hit, we huddled inside the house with nothing to do but wait for it to pass. The fine dust particles soon entered the house, and I remember that breathing became more difficult. As a "mouth breather," I could soon feel the grit between my teeth. The sky grew dark — similar in color to late dusk or early dawn. We could only see twenty or thirty feet into the yard, and the young kids would become frightened.

As the storm raged, dust began to show up on every item in the house; even the inside of the closets did not escape. The curtains soon showed a brown tint, and as the storm progressed, became darker and darker until they were black. All dishes, eating utensils, pots and pans had to be rinsed. Mom impatiently cleaned things up, but since some of these storms lasted for several days, this early effort had little effect.

Finally, the storm subsided and we walked to school — if it were in session. We encountered small drifts of dust covering the sides of the road and in protected areas all over the landscape.

Kicking a drift provided a dusty billow as if a smoke bomb had been ignited. It was difficult to find water clear enough to drink. Dad carried a number of water buckets into the house, and Mom left them for a day or so for the dust to settle out of the murky water. When the dust finally settled, a thin brown layer could be clearly seen on the bottom of the bucket. It took weeks for the dusty evidence to disappear — and a good rain was the best cleanser.

A dust storm on the way.

Better hurry!

❧ 48 ❧

Dust Devils

Off in the distance, I can see it coming. I throw down my hoe and run to where I think it is going. As I get close to it, I can see a wall of dust swirling directly in front of me. I dance with it for a few yards before I make the jump through the wall and try to keep up while inside. My clothes feel like they are being twisted around me. And then it is gone. Well, that was a nice interruption in this long, long day in the cornfield! We will talk about dust devils again tonight and then look forward to another one tomorrow.

Unlike the troublesome dust storms, we welcomed dust devils whenever they appeared. They usually showed up in the morning shortly after we got to the fields for hoeing or cultivating. Our best farmland was adjacent to the creek, and the dust devils most often formed over this area. They frequently appeared in pairs, sometimes dancing around each other, and twirling to heights of twenty to perhaps eighty feet.

When someone spotted a spinning dust spout, the kids ran as fast as possible to catch up with it. The lucky ones tried to stay inside the devil as long as possible until it disappeared in a chaotic puff. If other kids got close enough, they threw hands full of dust or grass into the swirl and watched it spin upwards.

We encountered dust devils on many occasions while driving along the road. Dad sometimes sped up or slowed down in hopes of making contact. I remember a few times when we caught up with one; it shook the car and dumped considerable debris inside, providing a very exciting experience.

We never knew exactly what caused these "little tornados," but Dad said that it had to do with the cool air over and along the creek. In the early morning, this cool air reacted with the hot air over the fields to form these small twisters. Scientists today affirm this theory, and I often wonder if Dad might have become a good scientist if his life had taken a different turn.

Fun in the distance ... dust devil!

❧ 49 ❧

Ice Skating on Shaw Creek

As I step on the ice, I hear a "pop" that reverberates around the bend and off into the distance. Dad says that this is caused by a break in the ice when we step on it, and the crack continues all the way to the end of the creek. This is a good sign that the ice is strong enough to hold me up. As the dirt wears off my shoes, I "skate" faster and faster.

Shaw creek ran through Pop's place and not only provided wonderful fishing and swimming in the summertime, but also ice-skating in the winter. From early December until late February, we had an opportunity to slip and slide for over a mile on this narrow, winding strip of ice. We proudly called this activity ice-skating, but we didn't have ice skates. We wore either our school or work shoes to slide on. A few adults, including my dad, had real ice skates. These attached to regular shoes with two metal clamps on the front and back and tightened with a skate key. To provide a little more support, Dad also wrapped a leather strap around his ankles and skates.

Although we occasionally played games together, including a dangerous ice-version of "crack-the-whip," most of the time we just skated up and down the creek. Trees and shrubs with branches bent over the ice surface. To complete the partial circle from under the bridge on the north side of the property to the bridge on the southwest side required walking across two narrow gravel barges that connected two ice-covered, deep-water holes.

Even with about twenty cousins skating at one time, we still found ourselves skating alone for rather long intervals. On one early fall afternoon, I slid around a bend and came upon my cousin, Don, who struggled in waist deep water after breaking through the ice. He called for me to help. I tried for a few minutes, but I just couldn't pull him out.

Our stories of the rescue attempt differ at this point, but I recall him yelling for me to run for help — so I ran all the way up to the house. Since it was a Sunday afternoon, the men played poker and the women washed dishes and visited. I stormed into the house shouting that Don had fallen through the ice and needed help right away. No one paid any attention to this seven-year-old. Perhaps I had yelled "wolf" too many times and no one believed me. It frightened me terribly. In later life, I had dreams where I would yell an emergency message to people who seemed to think I was invisible and did not hear me at all.

As it turned out, my cousin Darrell pulled Don out of the icy creek shortly after I ran for help. When they both arrived at the house — very wet and cold — the event finally registered with the adults. They exhibited great concern — but never attempted to explain why they ignored me.

Don's version explained that I saw his plight and, without any communication — and making no effort to get him out — made a beeline to the house for help. Yet, if Darrell had not arrived when he did, Don would probably not be around to offer me such wonderful tennis competition, walks on the beach, wagering on college basketball and e-mail companionship during our retirement years.

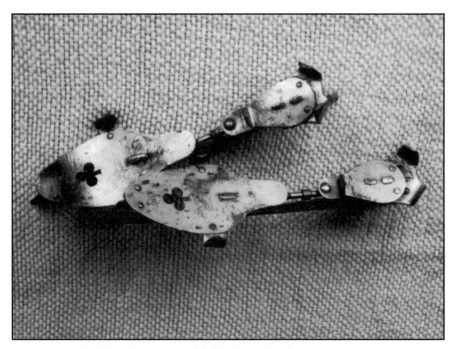

Dad's ice skates.

❧ 50 ❧

Dehorning and Degassing

Curley, come on. Stand up. My favorite cow is lying on her side and breathing very hard. I pet her and feel her soft curls of hair. She is the only cow I have ever seen with such a pretty coat. Dad is checking her over to see what is wrong. I know he will help her get well.

We dehorned cattle on a yearly basis. We accomplished this very difficult process by using a hand-held saw. Although we did this operation on many animals, we sometimes slipped and caught the calf's flesh at the base of the horn. Since the horn was living tissue, we always had some bleeding. A great deal of blood would occasionally be spilled if we cut too deeply into the base. We then put some terrible smelling tar-like ointment over the open gash on the cow's skull to keep out flies. If they got in, their eggs would hatch into maggots.

Maggots are difficult to describe to someone who has never seen one. They are slimy and white and constantly move together by the hundreds. While normally associated with dead carcasses, they cause great concern when observed on a live animal. When maggots appear, a meaner smelling liquid is applied to the cavity of the calf's horn, and sometimes the calf does not survive. I asked why we had to saw the horns off these animals. The answer was that it protected the other cattle from getting gored. I had never seen the theory tested with our own cattle, but did see other herds with lots of horns that showed no apparent ill effects. Sometimes the answer to our questions was "just because" and "that was that."

When I returned from school one day, I found my dad very upset. He had found that one of our prize cows had broken through a fence and had ventured into the alfalfa field. She had gorged herself with the sweet-smelling grass and collapsed to the ground. As she lay on the ground, her upper side was much larger than usual — bloated from gasses trapped inside her stomach. After unsuccessfully trying to get the cow upright, Dad finally ran into the house for a large butcher knife, then plunged it into the bloated side of the cow. With a great explosion of escaped gases, the cow arose to a standing position. The cow survived the ordeal after Dad cleaned the knife's puncture wound. Apparently this process isn't always successful, but this one provided a lasting memory.

A similar chemical reaction occurs if hay is baled when it is too wet. It may ferment to the point where it catches fire. I heard of barns burning down after they were filled with fresh bales of wet hay. After we filled the haymow with a fresh crop, we would "sample" a bale or two each day for several days. We tore them apart and placed our hands on the inside of the bale to check for excessive heat. When the bales were warm, the heat generated a little steam. Dad seemed to know if it were dangerous to leave the hay in the mow. On only one occasion did the alfalfa get hot enough to scare us into tossing the bales from the barn and breaking them apart. We hated that day when we waited several hours for the loose hay to dry — and then threw it back into the barn using "back-breaking" hayforks.

Curley.

✣ 51 ✣

Spatzies and Brass BBs

I take aim at the spatzie sitting on a low branch of the tree. He's all fluffed up, so he looks large in my sight. I pull the trigger, I hear the BB hit him, and he falls to the ground. I run over and pick him up; he is still breathing and blinking his eyes. I lay him down next to the tree and walk away trying to forget the sight.

Sparrows were a real problem around the farmhouse and the barn. Besides depositing droppings on everything, they stole chicken feed as well as cattle feed. My parents and grandparents called them "spatzies," so we kids did, too. Years later, I found that "spatzie" meant "little sparrow," and was one of the few German words that we all used on a daily basis. We were encouraged to kill them with our BB guns. Whether at school during the week, or at Sunday school, we compared our "spatsie-kill" totals on an almost daily basis. However, this was not always an easy assignment. Our guns were usually hand-me-downs — very old and in poor condition.

My BB gun was just a single-shot, although it looked impressive with a lever-action — just like the expensive multiple-shot models. I dropped a single BB down the barrel to load it for action. With such an old model, I had to keep the barrel pointed slightly upward while stalking my prey. This prevented the BB from rolling out, and also provided a little more safety.

With so many BBs flying around the farmyard, it was inevitable that one of us would occasionally get hit. I was walking into the house late one evening when something hit my right eye. Although I was not in much pain, I could feel it in my eye as I ran to Mom for help. She pulled up my eyelid and a BB fell out. This was another chance for Mom to warn me about "losing an eye," but was as close as any of us got to a serious injury from BBs or from other guns.

During World War II, when it was very difficult and expensive to acquire brass BBs, most of us had to settle for the cheaper lead BBs. The soft lead easily became off-round and would stick in the barrel, sometimes just dribbling out as I fired. Brass BBs, however, kept their shape and their trajectories were accurate and reliable.

My cousin, Don, who lived in town, visited Pop's place every Sunday with his parents and always had a new box or two of shiny brass BBs. He also had a state-of-the-art air-pump BB gun that was the envy of the entire clan of cousins. When any of the rest of us hit a spatzie, we heard a dull "thump" right before the bird dropped. When Don shot and hit one, with his high-powered gun, it was a sharp "splat."

We enjoyed as much target practice as possible with limited ammunition. A bale of hay was used as a back support for an old bottle or a paper target. When Don left the target area, we would scramble to find the used BBs in the hay bale. The lead BBs were seldom reused, but we retrieved as many of the brass ones as possible. In fact, I remember counting the number of times that Don shot his gun so that we would know exactly how many to look for. These recycled brass BBs were sometimes used over and over.

I never owned a full box of brass BBs until I purchased one as an adult. Pouring them out on the kitchen table stimulated wonderful memories. After purchasing an authentic single-shot BB gun from an antique store, I still feel a thrill when I roll a single brass BB down the barrel.

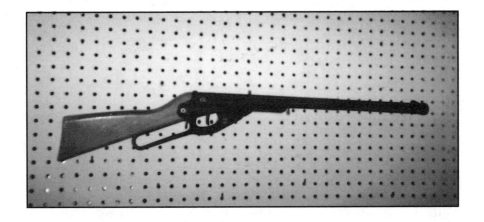

Spatzie killer!

❧ 52 ❧

Mice in the House and Gophers in the Field

As I walk out to get the cows, I spot several new dirt mounds. I kneel down and pick up a handful of the soft, warm soil. I let the dirt fall between my fingers, get up and start stomping around the opening. Dad will be unhappy when I tell him that the gophers are busy again.

By the time I arrived on the farm, we rode horses mostly for fun and not as an important part of our farm program. Several years earlier, on nearly open range, the safety of riding horses, as well as the safety of the cattle themselves, was constantly in mind. With the discovery of new soft mounds of dirt in our pastures, and the associated deep holes in the ground, an obvious danger was still present. My dad and Pop devised a number of plans to get rid of the culprits. These holes linked entry ways to vast tunnels dug by pocket gophers — although prairie dogs and badgers also caused problems. Gophers look like big rats, but with shorter tails. They were our enemies and we had to eliminate them.

Although currently very popular, gopher and prairie dog shooting was not a common sport in those days. The reason, most likely, was the high cost of war-time ammunition. We hauled large tubs of water to the location of the colony and poured it into the holes. We also tried to kill the gophers by placing a hose from the exhaust pipe on our car into the holes. This, of course, was a major project in the days before duct tape, as well as the difficulty of getting the car into the hills and near the site. I remember Dad taking a large pry-bar and angrily pounding the ground over the tunnels until they caved in. This was quite futile, but seemed to help Dad's mood a little.

Perhaps we saw some improvement after each of these efforts, but it was not measurable. At times, it seemed like even more varmints would show up within a few weeks after one of our attempts to get rid of them.

Another pest problem was partially solved using one of Dad's tricks that I have not heard of since. Dad worked it on hundreds of mice in our barn and granaries. He placed a 55-gallon barrel, almost filled with water, in a strategic spot and sprinkled ground cattle or chicken feed over the water surface — held in place by surface tension. With the mice, and sometimes a rat, thinking that this was a full barrel of very fine food, they would jump in and drown. I remember my dad straining dozens of mice out of the barrel over a period of many days. Over the next several weeks, we saw a significant decrease in the mouse population, and with the assistance of our large number of cats, it might be sustained for several weeks. However, the mouse population eventually began to rise again and the whole procedure would have to be repeated.

We used single-baited mousetraps in our house and kept the numbers down to the point of not being any more than a nuisance. This could probably be attributed to Mom's determined house-cleaning and protection of food supplies. Whenever we spotted a mouse, Mom set a trap and most often, by the next morning, we caught the mouse. Surprisingly, the nightly activity of mice running within the walls and ceilings of our house was not affected much even if we did capture several in traps. They must have had their own food supply and were safe from weather and cats as long as they stayed between the walls.

"Those dad-gummed gophers!"

🌿 53 🌿

115 Degrees and Canning

By late summer afternoon the temperature is soaring. Several gallons of water have been boiling on the wood-burning kitchen stove since early morning. Dozens of pint and quart jars are immersed in the boiling water — waiting to be filled with several different vegetables and fruits. Lids and rubber gaskets are also being sterilized in hot water. Boy, is it hot in here!

The canning process usually lasted from several days to two weeks. A wide range of vegetables including beets, corn, turnips, tomatoes, green beans, peas and carrots — as well as jams and jellies — were prepared for the canning process. Mom generally worked alone during the long days — peeling, slicing and dicing on the wooden cabinet top.

A Sunday school classmate had been badly burned a few years before I moved to the farm. A bucket of boiling water somehow slipped from the kitchen stove and burned the right side of her face, shoulder and side. It was a difficult and painful healing process and Mom reminded us of it often. So, on canning days, Mom said, "Stay outside and don't bother me."

Tomatoes were probably the most popular of the canning items. We harvested several bushels each year, and they provided a significant part of our home-canned goods. This process did not require an expensive pressure cooker — which was fortunate since we only had a small one for producing limited quantities of specialty food items.

The first step involved pouring boiling water over several dozen tomatoes and then, after a minute or two, plunging them into cold water for a few seconds. The skin slipped off easily and the bare tomatoes were ready to be canned. A few empty jars were placed upside down to drain on cotton cloths resting on the kitchen table. Within a few minutes, the tomatoes were carefully packed into these hot, scalded jars. The canning jar was filled to within a few inches of the top with an added teaspoon of salt. The rubber gaskets and lids were retrieved from the hot water and loosely fitted to the top of the jar. Six to eight filled jars were then placed inside a large pan and left to boil for a few hours. The water inside the tomatoes boiled out to fill the jar. Then, using metal prongs, the jars were removed and the lids tightened and left to cool.

Each of the various vegetables and fruits had a unique canning technique which Mom had memorized. I do not remember Mom using printed recipes for any of her cooking over the years. With the final completion of the canning process, the beautiful, glistening jars would be stored on rows along the eight-foot long shelves in the pantry. The pantry was located as an inside room next to the kitchen. With shelves on three walls from floor to ceiling, the shiny glass jars almost provided a light of their own. No bank vault had a greater treasure than this wonderful room. Along with potatoes and crock-pots full of pork chops and sausages, packed in lard, we could now face the long winter ahead.

Sparkling Ball jars for canning.

❧ 54 ❧

Wash Days

It's wash day! Mom and I walk from the washhouse to the back-yard to hang up the clothes. Mom is carrying the wet clothes in a basket. She takes an old wet rag off the top of the clothes pile and drags it along the full length of the wires to be sure they are clean and will not leave a streak on the clothes. It is kind of fun to hand her the wash, one at a time, as she clips them to the wire with wooden clothespins.

The move from the peaceful oil-lease home near Winfield, Kansas, to the rather harsh homestead of my grandfather required sacrifices in all aspects of daily life. One positive change, however, was getting to use the "monster" clothes-washing machine that Pop had invented. We had used a hand washboard up to that time. Pop's machine, however, ran off a two-horsepower gasoline engine with an eight-foot-long rubber drive-belt!

Once we started the engine, the large tub and rotating assembly inside were engaged by using a hand lever to operate a clutch mechanism. The contraption was housed in our "wash house" — a small wood frame building, with a dirt floor. We had to stake the machine to the ground to keep it from vibrating so violently the belt would fly off.

Only the toughest and dirtiest clothes were washed this way

since they took a major beating in the cleaning process. Of course, on an active farm like ours, and with everyone laboring in dust and heat day after day, we had substantial washing requirements. The engine ran at only one speed, and when we thought the clothes were clean, we released the clutch to shut the engine down. We often found the homemade lye soap not sufficient enough to "cut the dirt," so we added additional soap to the washer and made attempts to re-start the hot engine. The engine generally had to cool off for several minutes before starting again — so the wash day then extended into the afternoon hours.

On one occasion, after Dad had an accident while working under the tractor, his overalls were saturated with oil. Mom put them, along with a few other dark clothes, into the big washing machine, and after an hour of running, stopped the engine. She lifted out the clothes and found that the oil had permeated the entire inside mechanism. The thin film of oil seemed to be permanent, and only after several hours of hard scrubbing did some of it come off. After that, the clothes did not wash as well and the machine was used less frequently. It was back to the washboard!

To the kids in my school, helping with the washing, using a washboard, was similar to winding the home-made ice cream freezer. Both were terribly boring, but working with the washboard never had such a happy ending. We sat outside on a large flat rock with the washboard held upright in a tub of warm, soapy water. Mom brought clothes out one at a time and told us to rub them over the undulations of the washboard until she declared them clean. This might take only a few minutes; in some cases, it seemed like we were washing for hours. She, of course, completed most of the wash in her washtub inside the washroom.

In nearly all kinds of weather, the wet clothes hung on an

outside wire clothesline. Although we tried to gather them in before sundown, in the wintertime they were often frozen to the line. Mom said if we tried to remove them and/or bend them while carrying, they would actually break into pieces. I never saw that event but, on the other hand, we never tried it. We would leave them on the line — sometimes for several days — until they thawed out.

We wore overalls daily — at least for a full week before washing them. The t-shirts in the summer time were changed a little more often, but flannel shirts in the winter were also worn for a week or more before washing. Now, well into adulthood, I remember these childhood experiences and still try to be very conservative with how long I wear my clothes before dumping them into the laundry chute.

Back to the washboard.

🌿 55 🌿

Picnics on Sharpes Creek

What a beautiful place! The shallow creek looks almost white when the water splashes over the rocks. This hot summer day changes quickly as we get out of the car and spread a blanket under the large walnut trees. The flowing water feels so good on my bare feet. We'll wade, swim and fish during the long afternoon.

On very rare occasions, perhaps once or twice each summer, the entire family packed early in the morning and drove to a very beautiful picnic spot about ten miles to the southwest. The gravel road crossed through the shallow creek and over a thick layer of sandstone. Some fifty feet wide, but only about six inches deep, the creek offered a terrific setting for wading and just listening to the ripple of the water.

We had walnut and oak trees on our farm, but they could not compare to those gigantic ones on either side of Sharpes Creek. They provided a continuous arch or canopy over the whole scene. It was truly an oasis — even during the hot, dry days of July and August. The ground leading to the creek gently sloped and offered a smooth area to spread picnic blankets.

We did not want too many in our group; nor could they make too much noise since the owner of the land was very protective.

We learned not to ask for permission to have our picnics as he always turned us down. But if he did show up, although he would make quite a fuss, he allowed us to stay for the rest of the day. Rumor had it that he threatened a group with a rifle during one of their visits.

The morning hours were filled with carefree running and playing in the shallow water. Mom and Dad joined us for a few happy moments before preparing the picnic on the ground near the creek. With an unlimited rock supply, we carefully chose round, flat stones to skip over the length of the creek. The kid who could skip a rock the most times was declared the winner. I recall that seven skips almost guaranteed a win.

During the afternoon we relaxed after a full lunch. The adults either took naps on the picnic blankets or searched the creek for a promising fishing hole. We also took short walks to look for trees that had good crops of walnuts hanging from their limbs.

The trees along the creek produced great quantities of walnuts in the fall, and we walked along the roadside and quickly picked up several gunnysacks full. Along with those we picked up on the home place, we now had a rich supply that lasted throughout the rest of the year.

We emptied our walnut sacks on the ground and on flat rocks in the yard and spread them out in the sun. After several days, the outside layer dried and we broke it off with our hands. This left the walnut to dry for at least several more days until it was ready to break open. Dad tried all kinds of methods, but the best way was to place each walnut on a heavy iron pad and break it open with a hammer. The broken pieces of the hard shell, along with the meat, were thrown into a bucket for Mom and the kids to eventually separate.

As the fall progressed and the weather turned cold, we spent what spare time we had "picking" the walnuts. The goal was to have a good quantity available for Thanksgiving and Christmas. We also occasionally found a small handful of walnuts in our lunch buckets at school. Some kids had a cup full or more — making up the biggest part of their lunch.

In later years, Mom either bought or was given walnuts to crack open and pick, and this provided a very relaxing activity for her. Memories of the wonderful Sharpes Creek picnics surely crossed her mind.

Under the cool trees on Sharpes Creek.

56

Three Over Two

Ring, Ring, Ring, Riiiiing, Riiiiing. "Mom, Mom, it's our number," I shout. Mom runs in from the outside milk room, drying her hands with a towel. She reaches the phone high on the wall in the kitchen, takes the receiver off its cradle, cups her hand over the mouthpiece and shouts, "Hello, hello." Pause. "Oh, I was just out cleaning the separator, what are you doing?" She obviously is answering the same question that callers always ask: "What are you doing?"

A phone call really lightened up the day, and every kid dreamed of talking on that magic machine — even if it were only a few words. Our six-party line included the Joneses, two Gramke families, Uncle Walt and Aunt Martha Schroeder, the Mockerys and us. It did not take long to recognize the rings of the other parties, as well as our own three shorts and two longs. To call someone on our party line, we cranked the correct series of rings with the handle on the right side of the telephone box. The actual number assigned to each of the parties was shortened to the number of shorts followed by the number of longs and expressed, for our number, as "three over two."

The phone lines rarely permitted clear and steady communication. Not only was there a constant buzzing but, to be heard at all, required shouting every word.

The Stuttles, up the road, were responsible for the upkeep on the telephone lines for the district. Not only did Mr. Stuttle work on the poles and lines, Mrs. Stuttle functioned as the main operator in the nearby town of Olpe.

The telephone lines reacted to variations in weather. Ice caused the main worry, snow and wind also posing a concern. During each winter, we could expect the lines to "be down" several times, but generally for no longer than a few days. In addition to use in emergencies, the telephone was a social contact between families who lived several miles apart. To make a call outside the district, a single long was cranked on our telephone to get the operator. When she answered, we would give her the number we were calling and she would connect the call and record a fee. This fee was paid at the end of each month, along with the regular phone bill.

The central office in Olpe was located in a residential house at the north end of Main Street. The operator was occasionally called and asked to look out the window to see if someone's car were parked in front of the pool hall or the grocery store. She answered politely and occasionally provided more information than asked for. On a few occasions, a farmer missed a number of his regular pool games because of these reports.

In case of an emergency such as a prairie or home fire, accident or weather warning, the operator sent out a single long ring to all customers. When the ring was answered, the operator would share the details about the emergency. Other shared uses were not so well tolerated.

Even with small groups, such as a half-dozen families on party lines, there seemed to be social and personal conflicts. When a number rang, it sounded in all party-line homes and, although answered by the targeted party, many times others would listen in, too. If one listened closely, noises from other homes could sometimes be heard, and it would be evident that the conversation was not private. I remember Mom telling Mabel to "get off the line — this is not your call!" But Mom listened in on other conversations as well. Sometimes those listening in actually joined the welcomed conversation. Occasionally problems occurred when kids were at home and the parents worked outside. Some cruelly clicked the cradle of the receiver to make popping sounds over the lines. They would further disturb the parties with screams, yells and laughter. Of course, it was pretty easy to trace down these culprits, and their parents generally exerted some kind of serious discipline.

On one hot summer day, my sister, my cousin and I found ourselves alone in the house when the phone began to ring. We looked at each other for a moment and I decided to answer. I did not identify myself and made some wisecracks to the caller. Then I laughed and handed the phone over to Bonnie who made some chicken sounds. Lloyd then took over and mooed like a cow. He hung up quickly, but we soon knew we were in trouble. It was only a matter of time before this misbehavior was relayed to our parents. Later that afternoon, Mom found out!

The magic box high on the wall.

Present-day home of Rural Central.

ॐ 57 ॐ

Climbing the Windmill

The phone is ringing and I know who it is this time. Mom answers and sounds furious. My sister, Bonnie, and my visiting cousin, Lloyd, and I have been playing with the telephone and probably did some things we should not have done. Bonnie takes off in one direction and Lloyd and I run down by the creek. We know we are in trouble, but perhaps if we can hide for a while, Mom will cool off. Maybe it is time to get the nerve to climb to the platform at the top of the windmill.

Climbing windmills was a great challenge to many of us. As farm kids grew older, they usually kept trying until they eventually got to the top. It generally took until about the fourth grade to make it, but on this particular day, we two second-graders were going to give it our best shot. The windmill had not pumped water that day and was silently motionless for our ascent.

We had heard that the climb up was the easy part — just do not look down. We also heard that getting down was by far more difficult. Lloyd started up first, and I followed. We had rehearsed for this day many times; we had carefully practiced climbing the first few rungs on the ladder and then, looking down, carefully backtracked. Now, more determined than ever, we inched upwards, one step at a time, until we reached the edge of the platform near the top. Lloyd disappeared through the opening and I was to go next. Still not looking down and hanging on tightly to the side rails, I found that I had to release at least one hand to start my exit to the platform. I was paralyzed with fear before I finally held on extra hard with my left hand and extended my right arm and then the rest of my body through the opening. Lloyd crept to the other side as I crawled onto the wooden deck holding tightly to the sides. Several minutes went by until I got the courage to look around. Lloyd, by now, was quite comfortable,and he described all kinds of things in his view from the top. He actually sat on the edge of the platform with his feet dangling over the side. But I could not move my body any farther toward the edge. My only thought was that I would have to climb down, and I could not imagine how I would do it.

Mom apparently gave up looking for us, and that seemed like a mixed blessing. I would really have welcomed the sight of her — even if it meant some sort of punishment for the telephone mishap. Finally, after what seemed like hours, Lloyd suggested it was time to climb down. I had still not moved except to look closely at the mechanism of the fans and gears very near my head. What a complicated device! I wondered how anyone could build something like that.

The climb down frightened me. Going back through the opening was most difficult, but hanging tightly to the side rails eased my step-by-step descent. Once down, I was so relieved; I never made another trip to the top of a windmill until some ten years later. When we moved to another farm, I climbed to the top of the windmill to attach a TV antenna and managed the job with vivid memories of my previous climb, but with not as much fear.

Upon arriving back home, Mom soundly scolded us for just a few minutes, and then told us to do the chores. At least I then knew how the farm and near countryside looked from a bird's eye view. Even after 60 years, the feelings of helplessness when on the platform near the fan reappear in dreams of my childhood days.

A high climb.

✿ 58 ✿

July 4th

The sun is shining through the bedroom window. I awake even before Mom comes up the stairs. It sure is easier to get up on these bright warm mornings than it was during the school year. I think I will get up and start on my chores. Wait a minute — this is the 4th of July! By the time the milking is done and the calves and pigs are fed, my cousins will arrive. I check the top of the dresser; there is my block of a few hundred ladyfingers wrapped in a bright red package. This is going to be a great day!

Since Independence Day is a summer holiday, its history and meaning were only lightly addressed in the second grade curriculum. I overheard recitations by the older kids about our war with England back in the 1700s, but I did not have a grasp of the real meaning of July 4th celebrations. We would draw and color United States flags and attempt to fit in the forty-eight stars on the blue background. We could take the drawings home, but they were either lost or misplaced by the time July came around.

Our celebration of July 4th was not so much for Independence Day, but for Pop's birthday. Born in 1875, he had arrived from Germany with his parents and, in 1887, began to farm in the Stony Ridge community. As the years went by, my Uncle Sam married Dorothy whose birthday was also on July 4th. A few years later, cousin Don was born on July 4th. So, with three July 4th birthdays, this tradition was even more enhanced. Since then, we have had additional July 4th birthdays so that, since Pop's time, each generation is represented.

These celebration days resembled our regular Sunday family gatherings on the farm, except that, if we did not go to church on that day, people arrived much earlier. The adults paused to remember, with pride, the purpose of the day. But the kids spent the time lighting firecrackers and anticipating fireworks later that evening. Since we had to work the next day, the nighttime fireworks started as soon as daylight began to fade. The kids tried to talk the adults into an early start all during the afternoon.

Our noon meal — called dinner — was served in the kitchen, cafeteria style. If the weather were good, everyone fanned out over the grounds outside looking for a shady spot to eat. Soft drinks were unavailable, but we had an unlimited supply of milk and, of course, beer was available for the adults.

As the special guest of honor, Pop often walked by and stopped for a few minutes to talk to each group scattered over the grounds. I recall him as being very humble and friendly with everyone. Our respect and reverence for him was very evident. If I, or any of my cousins, could get a minute or two with him, we were delighted. He would place his hand on our heads, rub our hair lightly, and speak softly to us. After visiting an hour or two, he disappeared into his bedroom, next to the living room, for an afternoon nap.

Cousin Don was the other hero of the day for the kids. We waited anxiously for him to arrive with his parents from town. We had only a limited supply of fireworks, consisting mostly of very small firecrackers called ladyfingers. The little kids ran around waving the wire handles of fiery sparklers. Don, however, unloaded a supply of the most modern fireworks available. He was in the next highest age group of cousins, and he shared the prizes with those of his own age. The rest of us might get to fire an occasional cherry bomb or an even larger two-and-a-half or three-inch firecracker. We just watched in awe as the older kids lighted those magnificent explosives, the sounds reverberating throughout the countryside. Torpedoes were especially popular as they exploded on impact when thrown against any hard surface. The feet of the little kids made easy targets, and sometimes we danced away quickly when one exploded nearby.

Finally, when the sun sank in the west, some of the adults or much older cousins brought out the popular roman candles. These were long cardboard tubes that propelled red, blue, green and yellow fireballs into the sky. Safety concerns caused everyone to carefully place the candles in the ground before firing them upward. When they sometimes became more daring, the candles were held in a hand and directed either upwards or along an angle into the sky. On one occasion, a candle backfired and the fireball ran up the sleeve of cousin Wayne and found a resting spot in his armpit. After such a painful experience, the firing became more conservative — at least for that one July 4th!

The end of the day came all too fast after so much anticipation. And the prospect of this kind of fun for the rest of the summer dimmed considerably. It would be back into the fields again tomorrow with endless hot days ahead!

Little kids with sparklers.

59

The Move to Town

"Better go to the bathroom now — you need to leave in a few minutes," Mom said. I think this will be a short walk for me since the school is only five blocks from home. How strange to be carrying my lunch in a paper sack instead of my syrup can! But that's what the letter said! The letter also said that school began at 8:30 and that my room is number 211, on the second floor. I have never had this feeling before! It is cloudy and cool, but I am sweating and really have to go to the bathroom, again. Wow, this is what people call "being nervous!" I'm not sure I will make it!

Toward the end of my last year in a one-room rural school, my dad became very ill with pneumonia. His recovery was very slow and it became necessary to sell the eighty-acre farm and move to town. We had a buyer within a few days and, almost before I knew what happened, I was walking up to a new school as large as our hay barn. One of the kids told me that we had to wait for the bell to ring before we went in. Once inside, I quickly found a bathroom. Along the walls were several urinals and open toilet stalls. What an unusual sight! I then went up to my room and walked in. I had never seen so many kids in one place as in that thirty-student classroom.

I do not remember being introduced to the class, but I was assigned a seat at the very back of the classroom. I completed my first class assignment very quickly and, as I had always done in rural schools, walked to the front carrying my paper and placed it on the teacher's desk. That was a mistake! Miss Hart informed me, "We don't do things that way in this school." My world changed at that point. I carried my paper back to my desk and waited in embarrassed silence.

I found out that my assignments would be graded by either the student ahead of or behind me. This time we handed the papers to the back. Since I was on the back of the row, it took a little coaching from the other kids to find out the student in that seat had to take their paper to the one in the front seat. Again, I took the lonely walk to the front of the room. The correct answers were read by the teacher, and the scores of each were sounded loudly back to her as she recorded them at the front desk. Although I had never seen this done before, it bothered me. But it was to be the standard procedure throughout the rest of my public school experience!

Making a few new friends proved easy enough, although the combination of my country overalls and, especially, my clodhoppers provided some derision for many of my classmates. I mentioned to my parents that I wanted some new clothes like the rest of the kids. But I had no chance of anything "new." Dad recovered from his illness and found a job carpentering with a couple of independent house builders. After taking a financial loss on the sale of the farm, we now started the very slow process of getting out of debt.

With continued problems of adjustment to my new school, my interest steadily declined. I started to miss an occasional day or two of school with a "stomach ache." This eventually led to absences lasting for several days at a time.

I had recently made a friend, living near my house, who was two years older than me who made regular visits to the public library just a few blocks away. He invited me to join him one day, and what a revelation I received! From the moment I first walked into that great building, I was hooked for life! Books were on shelves, from the floor to the glass ceiling, and they lined the walls forming row after row of islands with narrow aisles. My friend, David, showed me a narrow stairway near the back that we crept up and discovered the glass ceiling formed the floor of a entire second story of books. The librarians seemed so happy to see me, and they gave me directions to find books of great adventure and excitement.

With the discovery of the library and the privilege of borrowing up to three books at a time, I totally escaped the rest of the world for the remaining weeks of that spring. Using a little gas space heater for heat and light, I would lie on the floor and read for hours at a time — and I attended school only with great pressure from my parents.

I passed third grade, probably because of my grades and recommendations from the Stony Ridge teacher and, during the summer, we moved "south of the tracks" to another school district. That fall I met a teacher who had the same commitment and compassion as my previous rural-school teachers. Mrs. Berg somehow found me and guided me through a wonderful fourth grade year. So, after only a few months interruption, I began my way again to find fun and success in academic life.

Bigger than our barn!

60

The Wall

I drive up the familiar lane and cannot believe my eyes. At the far end, near the house, is a magnificent series of a half-dozen rocks standing vertically out of the ground. They extend to eight feet high and form an arched line along the roadside. Several relatives are already lounging around on benches and chairs. Cousin Gilbert greets me at the side of the car with a handshake and says, "Kenny, I've got to show you something."

After being away for almost fifty years, I returned to the Schroeder home place to attend a family reunion. Gilbert had purchased the farm many years earlier and had started a full-time project that would take over six years to complete.

The long, gentle curve of the lane leading from the main road to the house has changed significantly. It has metamorphosed to an exciting display of more than one hundred limestone monoliths, with a combined weight of one thousand tons or more. Fitting together side by side, each of these stones possesses a unique size and shape and is filled with fossils millions of years old.

My cousin, Gib, built this magnificent structure by freeing limestone slabs from outcroppings on his pastureland and dragging them to the site from about three miles away. One by one, as the years went by, Gib, sometimes with the assistance of his sons, dug trenches by hand and fitted the stones into place using very little mechanical assistance. Thick layers of sandstone were found just a few feet below the surface and had to be removed using a pick and shovel. Even so, most of the stones in the wall are buried so deeply that nearly half of their length is underground.

I have escorted many visitors to view this site, including a few geology and history professors, who have seen other stone structures in the world. One stopped, took off his hat and said, "Absolutely incredible. Unless a major highway runs through this area, these stones could be here a thousand years or more."

The hard work, determination and creative engineering of this project speaks well for my cousin's effort. But, more importantly, it gives the entire family a real feeling that our home place will stand with honor for many generations to come. Perhaps Pop's farm will continue to be owned by one of his descendants. Grandkids will then have the opportunity to run from the farmhouse to the creek and into the pastures. I wonder if they will relate to "how things were" for their grandparents as they envision fishing, swimming and ice skating on Shaw creek, prairie baseball and hunting for spatzies?

The wall.